Single Mom???
What Now???

Endorsements

I have known Vicki since the early 1970's when we served the Lord together in Shiloh Youth Revival Centers. Vicki was and is a caring nurturer in the church of God. The single parent experience of those days most certainly has made her a subject matter expert. The fruit of her labor, her grown children, and friends testify to the same. As I read her prose, I see continuing demonstration of this truth.

Keith Kramis
Elder, Harvest Fellowship Community Church
Ordained Pastor and Minister, Shiloh Youth Revival Centers, Inc.

If you are (or know) a single parent, we heartily encourage you to read Vicki's new book! As Shiloh alums with Vicki from the 1970's, we read with joy her insights and stories. As one of many bona-fide single moms from those early ministry days (now happily married 35+ years), I remember many discussions, Scriptures, tears, and prayers we all shared across Shiloh office space, in living rooms, backyards, kitchens, children's bedrooms...wherever we would find ourselves melting down or standing in faith. The Lord was compassionately working His Word into our lives and families, and Vicki has skillfully and wisely brought her insights and lessons together in these pages.

Barb Moore
Support Staff, InterVarsity Christian Fellowship's National Service Center Support Staff in Central America,
Wycliffe Bible Translators

Mike Moore
Ordained Minister, Administrative Pastor,
Faith Community Bible Church
Support Staff in Central America, Wycliffe Bible Translators

Single Mom???
What Now???

Overcoming the Challenges...
A Single Mother's Journey

By Victoria Harr

Single Mom???
What Now???

Copyright © 2012 by Victoria Harr
ISBN 978-1-61529-063-5

For information on ordering please contact:
Vision Publishing
1672 Main St. E 109
Ramona, CA 92065
1-800-9-VISION
www.booksbyvision.com

All rights in this book are reserved world-wide. No part of this book may be reproduced in any manner whatsoever without written permission of the author, except in brief quotations embodied in critical articles of review.

All Scripture quotations, unless otherwise specified, are taken from the King James Version of the Bible. (Copyright © 1982 by Holman Bible Publishers. All rights reserved.)

Scripture quotations noted NKJV are from the *Holy Bible*, New King James Version, (Copyright © 1979, 1980, 1982 by Thomas Nelson, Inc. Used by permission. All rights reserved.)

Scripture quotations noted NASB are from the *Holy Bible*, New American Standard Bible, (Copyright © 1960, 1962, 1963, 1968, 1971, 1972, 1973, 1975, 1977, 1995 by The Lockman Foundation. Used by permission. All rights reserved.)

Scripture quotations noted NIV are from the *Holy Bible*, New International Version, (Copyright © 1973, 1978, 1984 by International Bible Society. Used by permission.)

Scripture quotations noted NLT are from the *Holy Bible*, New Living Translation, (Copyright © 1996. Used by permission of Tyndale House Publishers, Inc., Wheaton, Illinois 60189. All rights reserved.)

Transcribed from: The Holy Bible: Revised Standard Version containing the Old and New Testaments, translated from the original tongues: being the version set forth A.D. 1611, revised A.D. 1881-1885 and A.D. 1901: compared with the most ancient authorities and revised A.D. 1946-52. —2nd ed. of New Testament A.D. 1971.

DEDICATION

When I wrote my first book, I knew I had three books on my heart to write, and I knew what the topics would be about: spiritual gifts, passing on a grandmother's legacy, and single mothers. That is why my third book is dedicated to all the single mothers I lived with and have known through the years who have taught me so much.

ACKNOWLEDGEMENTS

Rhonda Aydlett for sharing her heart while creating the cover design;

Kathleen Hays for invaluable input while proofreading through the eyes of a single mother;

Juanita Sutterfield for being a sounding board for different titles and cover designs;

All my brothers and sisters-in-the-Lord who prayed for me throughout the years I was living this book and later as I was writing it,

and finally for my husband, Sid, for not letting me give up.

TABLE OF CONTENTS

Introduction 8

Chapter 1: God's Promises 11
    A Single Mom's Christian Home
    God's Promises to Single Mothers
    Attitudes and Choices

Chapter 2: Spiritual Perspectives 27
    Faith: In What or Who?
    The God of Second Chances

Chapter 3: Trials and Tribulations 39
    Forgiving Your "Ex"
    Self-Worth/Self-Image
    Snares and Traps
    Priorities
    Coping
    Stress
    Periods/Hormones/Cycle of Emotions
    Suicidal Tendencies/Depression
    Soul Ties
    Generational Sins

Chapter 4: Navigating the Divorce/Separation Process 67
    To Reconcile or Not? – A Good Question
    Incentive to Reconciliation
    The Grieving Process
    Divorce
    Practical Stages and Their Emotional Counterparts
    Six Stages of Divorce

Chapter 5: Life After Divorce 95
    Preparation for Marriage or Remarriage
    Dating
    Engagement

Chapter 6: Life as a Single Mom 113
    Unusual Situations and Solutions
    A Fish Out of Water?
    A Single Grandmother
    Finding a Church
    Spiritual Counsel
    Spiritual Authority
    Financial Conditions
    Repairing Things That Break
    Holidays
    Common Questions During the Adjustment Period
    Never Married?
    Personal Ministry of Single Moms
    Your Personal Vision for the Future

Chapter 7: Friends 141
    Your Physical (Non-Sexual) Needs
    New Friends
    Opposite Sex Relationships Other Than Dating

Chapter 8: Children 149
    Children's Special Issues
    Children Asking Why
    Children's Curiosity About the Other Parent
    Children's Salvation
    Mutual Role Models for the Single Mother and Child
    Role Models/Big Brothers/Big Sisters for the Child
    Disciplining Challenges

Chapter 9: A Final Reflection 165

INTRODUCTION

The probabilities of you having been a single mother, presently being a single mother, or knowing a single mother are very high.[1] According to the 2006 U.S. Census Report, the number of single moms has remained constant at about 9.8 million, while the number of single dads grew by 25 percent in the decade between 1990 and 2000. In 2007, there were 20 million children in the U.S. under age 18 who had only one parent; 84% of those lived with their mothers.[2] Over 65% of Americans are now a stepparent, a stepchild, a stepsibling, a step-grandparent, or are touched directly by a stepfamily scenario.[3] In 2010, 41% of children were born to unmarried mothers.[4] Another way of looking at it is, "…over 24 million children in the United States today live apart from their biological father. That is one out of every three. It is even worse for African-American children. Nearly 50% of African-American boys and girls do not have a dad in the home."[5] Therefore, the odds of you being touched by a broken or blended family are a strong possibility indeed.

Although the times change and cultures are different, the Bible and the answers for most of the issues a single mother faces, do not. When one thinks of single mothers in the Bible, one is usually hard-pressed to immediately come up with an example. However, there are many stories about single mothers, and some of those women's lives will be studied in this book. God's promises were for them, and they are for you too.

This book is not meant to be primarily about parenting, or even about all the stages encountered when a parent leaves, such as divorce, separation, abandonment, or imprisonment. Instead, it focuses on those challenges specifically as they pertain to single mothers.

Many practical issues in this book will also apply to any parent or grandparent, regardless of sex or status. However, most of this book is directed to single moms since that was my journey.

Having been raised during my teenage years by a single mother, being a single mother myself for over five years with two young children, and then living communally with 30+ single moms for five years, I am personally acquainted with the unusual issues, trials, and tribulations that these single mothers and their children deal with. These problems and challenges are different than those encountered when one is married.

One day while thinking deeply about these things I had experienced, I asked myself, "From single mom to grandmother, where did the years go? How can I pass on any wisdom I have gleaned and the things I learned to the younger generation?" That is how and why this book was conceived.

CHAPTER 1

God's Promises

A SINGLE MOM'S CHRISTIAN HOME

So, you are a single mom now! Have you ever asked yourself, "What is a nice girl like me doing in a situation like this?" Well, I was certainly surprised when I found myself in this position. In fact, I was even embarrassed. I wondered, "What did I do wrong?" As a Christian, I was stunned! "How could this happen to me?" Somehow you have acquired the status of being a single mother, and to add to the awkwardness, you may be a Christian too. Perhaps you are a widow, never married, or maybe you have chosen to adopt as a single woman. However, it is more likely you have been divorced or deserted by your spouse.

In 2009, four in 10 children in America were *born* to single mothers.[6] That is almost 50%! That does not take into consideration the children who were initially born into a nuclear home[7] and are now being raised by a single mother. For that reason, I will refer to the partner in your prior relationship, whether you were married or not, as the other partner, the other parent, or your "ex."

Hopefully, somewhere along the way, Christ has entered your life as a new commitment or recommitment. However, He has not changed the circumstances of being alone and raising your family.

Well, cheer up! If you are serious about Jesus, about following His blueprint for your life, then your needs and life's direction will be different in many ways than if you were raising your family in a nuclear home or in a secular lifestyle.

First, let me establish the fact that in the Bible God talks a lot about widows, and He often refers to the fatherless, orphans, and widows in the same verse. In the Old Testament, a woman who was widowed was often set aside socially, considered discarded, and felt forsaken. In the New Testament, being a widow brings with it the idea of "having a vacancy through deficiency" (as in lacking a husband) [literally or figuratively].[8] This includes becoming a widow through death and can apply to a woman without a husband for whatever reason, with or without children.

Throughout the Bible, the term "fatherless" means "an orphan" or "without a father."[9] This indicates to me that the fatherless could be orphans without both parents, or could be fatherless and apply to children of single mothers, whether true widows, separated, divorced, or perhaps never married. Therefore, most of the verses which refer to "widows" in the Bible can be interchanged to read "single mothers," and the verses referring to "fatherless," and "orphans" can be interchanged to apply to children being raised by a single mother.

Now, let us look at some of the issues that single mothers uniquely deal with.

GOD'S PROMISES TO SINGLE MOTHERS

God's *love* IS NOT CONDITIONAL. He loves everyone the same. God's *promises*, however, are based upon certain conditions, so let us examine some of God's promises.

Single mothers and their children are uniquely special in God's heart. The foundation of how He views you as a single mother and His promises to you, are found in the following verses in Isaiah 54:4-17. Here God is speaking to the nation Israel about how He viewed them when they were walking in opposition to Him, and how He is going to restore them to Himself.

When I was a single mother, the Lord began speaking to me about how this chapter, beginning in verse 4, also applied to me in my situation as a single mother. This was a personal revelation to me at a specific time in my life; consequently, I personally dubbed it the "Single Mother's verses." I referred to this chapter over and over again during my five years as a single mom and was comforted in new ways each time.

Even though I read it with a personal mindset, I could see God's heart and promises for all single mothers. As you read it, ask the Lord to show you whether or not these promises apply to you as well.

When I have comments about the scripture verses, they are within brackets [ ] and are in **bold lettering**.

'Do not fear, for you will not be ashamed; Neither be disgraced, for you will not be put to shame;'

> *[Do not be fearful of being embarrassed, ashamed or confused by your status. He has already seen your circumstances and is putting steps in place to correct that situation. He is not surprised at your situation.]*

'For you will forget the shame of your youth, and will not remember the reproach of your widowhood anymore.'

> *[In hindsight, you will remember parts of what you went through, yet God promises the shame and reproachful feelings will eventually be gone if you embrace Him.]*

'For your Maker is your husband, The Lord of hosts is His name; and your Redeemer is the Holy One of Israel; He is called the God of the whole earth.'

> *[He created you. He made you for Himself. He wants you to experience as personal a relationship with you as a husband and wife can have, only more intimate because He is God. He wants you as His wife. Focus on the true meaning of "husband." Consider a husband's role. What does a husband do? What does a husband provide? Jesus will provide every need and fill every lack if you seek Him.]*

'For the Lord has called you like a woman forsaken and grieved in spirit, like a youthful wife when you were refused,' says your God.

> *[Being forsaken brings feelings of rejection and grief. A single mother has been abandoned on many different levels and often feels forsaken because she was refused and rejected by the love of her life, often when she was young and felt she had the best of herself to give.]*

'For a mere moment I have forsaken you, but with great mercies I will gather you.'

> *[This feeling of being forsaken is short-lived—only a "mere moment" in the big picture of our life and the larger perspective of eternity. God wants to replace those feelings with His mercy and love.]*

'With a little wrath I hid My face from you for a moment; but with everlasting kindness I will have mercy on you,' says the Lord, your Redeemer.

Chapter 1

> *[God turned his face from Israel temporarily, but He loved them so much that He could not "hide his face" from them for long. You may feel God is hidden from you right now; nevertheless, God promises He will show you His mercy and love.]*

'For this is like the waters of Noah to Me; for as I have sworn that the waters of Noah would no longer cover the earth, So have I sworn that I would not be angry with you, nor rebuke you.'

> *[In Genesis 9:8-17, after the flood, God gave us a sign in the form of a rainbow to remind us He would never destroy the world by water again. Whenever I see a rainbow, I am reminded that God will keep His promise not to discipline me in anger. He never wants to devastate a person. Instead when He steps in, He will handle each of His children personally, one-on-one, in the most appropriate way needed for each person.]*

'For the mountains shall depart and the hills be removed, but My kindness shall not depart from you, nor shall My covenant of peace be removed,' says the Lord, who has mercy on you.

> *[Even if the mountains were leveled and destroyed, He will deal with you with kindness, compassion, and peace that will not end. That is how much He cares for you.]*

'O you afflicted one, tossed with tempest, and not comforted, behold, I will lay your stones with colorful gems, and lay your foundations with sapphires.'

> *[You may be having sleepless nights and tearful days; however, regardless of how you presently feel, He promises to restore peace and beauty to your life. Although you may not feel comforted right now, you will.]*

'I will make your pinnacles of rubies, your gates of crystal, and all your walls of precious stones.'

> *[He knows a woman's heart. He knows she wants to feel beautiful, and He promises to build you up. He uses the language of colorful, precious, and valuable stones which are symbolic of your worth in His eyes. You are precious to Him. You are priceless in His eyes, just like these jewels are to mankind.]*

'All your children shall be taught by the Lord, and great shall be the peace of your children.'

[Your children have the ability to learn God's faithfulness and His nature from you. As they do this, they will receive peace even in the unsettled situation in which they find themselves.]

'In righteousness you shall be established; you shall be far from oppression, for you shall not fear; and from terror, for it shall not come near you.'

[You will be settled, solid, never wavering, stable, and hedged in by Him. You will be protected from fearful and terrible, oppressive things as His righteousness is imparted to you.]

'Indeed they shall surely assemble, but not because of Me. Whoever assembles against you shall fall for your sake.'

[Oppression and fear may attempt to come against you, but it is not what He desires for you. He will defeat them. Your enemies and problems will not continue to consume you, and they will disappear as you seek Him.]

'Behold, I have created the blacksmith who blows the coals in the fire, who brings forth an instrument for his work; and I have created the spoiler to destroy.'

[God has created each specific vessel (like the blacksmith) for a specific task (blowing coals for whatever type of metal or iron he is forming), and He created armies (the spoiler) for a specific purpose in Israel's history. He has also created you for a definite purpose. You may not yet know what that purpose is, but He has the answer for what you are dealing with, however it might look. Even if your life looks like a waste to you, He is molding it for your good. It was the same with Israel. Throughout history, Israel's enemies were used by God to bring Israel back to Him. God can use anything and everything to get your attention (even the unique things a single mom faces), because of His love for you. Israel was called to be His chosen people. You and your children are also called to be His chosen people.]

'No weapon formed against you shall prosper, and every tongue which rises against you in judgment you shall condemn. This is the heritage of the servants of the LORD, and their righteousness is from Me,' says the LORD (Isaiah 54:4-17 NKJV).

[No weapon intended to hurt you shall succeed. People who judge you and your situation will be silenced. Gossip

> *and judgment from others will be revealed for the lies that they are. You can expect God to work out everything for your good. As a child of God, these verses are your heritage and your inheritance.]*

As I read these verses, the Lord showed me I could choose to stay in a defeated mindset or choose to believe these promises. I decided to appropriate His promises, and I hope you will as well.

God also gives you promises about you *and* your children. If you store up the following verses from Deuteronomy 11 in your heart, God will bring you comfort, and you will receive the promises in verse 21. Whatever you are going through, He will give you a vision of your future destiny and a vision for your children's future too.

> 'Therefore you shall lay up these words of mine in your heart and in your soul, and bind them as a sign on your hand, and they shall be as frontlets between your eyes.'
>
>> *[If you are meditating on God's Word, it will be in your head and heart. As a result, God can recall those words to you when needed, bringing them to the forefront of your mind.]*
>
> 'You shall teach them to your children, speaking of them when you sit in your house, when you walk by the way, when you lie down, and when you rise up.'
>
>> *[You cannot teach something you do not know. Consequently, as you learn God's Word first, you are then able to continuously speak them in every situation in order to reinforce them to yourself and your children.]*
>
> 'And you shall write them on the doorposts of your house and on your gates,'
>
>> *[I used to find promises from the Lord out of His Word and write them on plaques or index cards or yellow sticky notes and put them around my house. Seeing them on the walls reminded me of what He had promised.]*
>
> 'that your days and the days of your children may be multiplied in the land of which the LORD swore to your fathers to give them...' (Deuteronomy 11:18-21 NKJV).

What a great thing to look forward to. Nevertheless, here are the choices and consequences if you choose not to follow Him.

> *'Behold, I [God] set before you today a blessing and a curse: the blessing, if you obey the commandments of the LORD your God which I command you today; and the curse, if you do not obey the commandments of the LORD your God, but turn aside from the way which I command you today, to go after other gods which you have not known' (Deuteronomy 11:26-28 NKJV).*

God's love is for everyone without conditions attached. God loves you just as you are, but He wants to bring you into a personal relationship with Him so you can receive and apply all His promises.

God's promises come with "Ifs." *If* you do what God asks of you, *then* God will fulfill His part. It is the principle of "If you," then "I, God."

This is the foundation you need to build on. God's hand is being held out to you. He is offering Himself to you in a very special way.

ATTITUDES AND CHOICES

Is being a single mom a privilege or a burden—a blessing or a curse? Are you going to be a victim or victorious? It is all in your attitude, in how you look at it. In each circumstance, you always have a choice. Look at the following verse.

> *Yet in all these things we are more than conquerors through Him who loved us (Romans 8:37 NKJV).*

You can be a survivor, or you can be "more than a conqueror" and overcome the obstacles that come your way.

Not all things that happen to us are good; nevertheless, as God's child, He will somehow weave the seemingly bad things in your life into good things if you (1) love Him, and (2) are called according to His purpose. The following verse is His promise to you.

> *And we know that all things work together for good to them that love God, to them who are the called according to [his] purpose (Romans 8:28 KJV).*

Chapter 1

Even when I was married, it was hard financially and emotionally, and as a single mother it was ever harder. When my perspective would become clouded by events in my life that would drag me down, I would feel burdened, and often I would even blame myself. I would feel like a failure. Maybe you feel like a failure right now. However, feelings are deceptive. You are not a failure. You are only a failure if you give up and quit.

Sometimes I *felt* like I was left to raise my children alone because of the absence of their father or fault of someone else. Then one day, I realized I was the mother who God specifically chose to raise these two particular children, even if I often *felt* it was by default. The truth was: This was NOT by default. He had entrusted me (not their father) with two souls that needed to be taught and guided as they launched out into this world.

Since I believe in a God who cares for me and who loves my children even more than I do, I believe it was no accident that these two unique children were given to me. In fact, God had chosen me to raise them *before* He even created the world.

> ...*just as He chose us in Him before the foundation of the world, that we should be holy and without blame before Him in love... (Ephesians 1:4 NKJV).*

Let that settle in...before He even created the world.

That is mind-boggling to me. I do not understand it; however, by faith I believe it. So, it was by *God's design*, not *man's default* that these children were mine to raise. Understanding the difference gave me a different perspective about my situation.

By the same token, you are the parent God *chose* to raise your child. He has *honored* you by allowing you to be the primary parent in this specific situation. You are the one He trusts; otherwise someone else would be raising your children.

No one chooses which family they will be born into—do they? And no one chooses the time in history where they will be born. Before you are born, no one has a choice where they will live. These situations are not random. God chooses the families and decides who belongs in each one, whether you are a single (solitary) person or married.

> *A father of the fatherless, a defender of widows, is God in His holy habitation. God sets the solitary [single] in families... (Psalm 68:5-6(a) NKJV).*

What is amazing to me is that He even establishes *when* people live in history as well as *where* they live geographically. This includes you.

> *...and He made from one man every nation of mankind to live on all the face of the earth, having determined their appointed times and the boundaries of their habitation... (Acts 17:26 NASB).*

> *...he will establish the border of the widow (Proverbs 15:25(b) KJV).*

During the times when I wanted to move geographically, He often kept me where I was until He knew it was the right time and He had prepared the right place for me to move. Once I understood it was because He had my best interests in mind, my attitude changed. I stopped being impatient and chafing at the bit to move. I did not always or even immediately see the reason for the delay, but I knew there was a higher purpose than just my wanting to move.

By the same token, in the larger scheme of things, God knows you are exactly the mother your child needs. It is not an accident, even if your child was a surprise. That may be a foreign concept to you. That thought may cause you to do a double-take, causing a major shift in your pattern of thinking about being a mother. By God's design you are precisely the mother your child needs. Understanding that alone can change your attitude.

He gave your children the exact temperament He wants for *you* to grow. They are like sandpaper on us to refine us, to change us to be more like Jesus.

Once I realized God considered me the best choice for my children, I was very encouraged, because at times I felt someone else could do a better job of raising my children. Perhaps you feel that way. I know I did. I knew I was good in my career as a legal secretary, but I was unsure in my role as a mother. Maybe you feel that way today. Perhaps you think a grandmother, babysitter or day care center can raise your child better. This probably stems from the messages our culture bombards us with and creates a lack of confidence in being a mother in general.

The other parent has not been responsible up to now. In spite of this, you are the one who has this very important responsibility, even if you feel it is by default. Nevertheless, it is still your decision whether to be bummed out, bitter, burdened, and look upon your circumstances as a curse, or instead, to recognize the fact that God *chose* YOU! The entire experience of being a single mother can be turned into a blessing by your attitude.

Do you know how special you are in God's sight? The following verse indicates how we should treat others, but it also commands others to treat you and your child in special ways.

> *Learn to do good. Seek justice. Help the oppressed. Defend the orphan. Fight for the rights of widows (Isaiah 1:17 NLT).*

Wow! He wants others to defend your child, to fight for your God-given rights, and to take up your cause on behalf of your child. Even more than that, He is your Advocate, He is your Defender, and your Interceder. It is a win-win situation.

The next verse shows how much He cares for you and how much He cares that others treat you right.

> *Defend the poor and fatherless; Do justice to the afflicted and needy. Deliver the poor and needy; Free them from the hand of the wicked (Psalm 82:3-4 NKJV).*

Does this describe your situation: being poor, children without a father, afflicted or needy? If so, take comfort in the fact that God is on your side. He is for you and He wants to see you blossom. He is your protector and will protect your children too. When speaking to Moses, the Lord said:

> *For the LORD your God is God of gods and Lord of lords, the great God, mighty and awesome, who shows no partiality nor takes a bribe. He administers justice for the fatherless and the widow, and loves the stranger, giving him food and clothing (Deuteronomy 10:17-18 NKJV).*

God is not partial and does not show favoritism. He is fair, and you cannot bribe Him into looking the other way when it comes to being just. You cannot bargain with Him or buy Him off. He will administer justice on your behalf in His timing.

God further admonishes others in how to treat you.

> *'You shall not afflict any widow or fatherless child. If you afflict them in any way, [and] they cry at all to Me, I will surely hear their cry...' (Exodus 22:22-23 NKJV).*

Even more than God hearing your cry, those who are against you will have to answer to Him. Listen to the strong language God uses.

> *Cursed is the one who perverts the justice due the stranger, the fatherless, and widow. And all the people shall say, 'Amen!' (Deuteronomy 27:19 NKJV).*

What a winning combination! You and God!

PERSONAL EXAMPLE: At one point I was struggling financially and I went to my pastor for counsel. After weighing all the possibilities, he suggested I move in temporarily with a married couple for financial reasons to make ends meet. Well, that answer made me feel worse, and I did not have a peace about it, but neither did I have any other solution. I just did not believe that would work in my situation with two older children. So I cried out to God to give me another solution because I felt even more afflicted. I read and believed the promise in Exodus 22:22-23, and God heard my cry. I was delivered financially in just a few weeks by a job promotion that was totally unexpected.

One story in I Kings 3 demonstrates King Solomon's Godly wisdom and justice towards two single mothers, one who was very devious. Each prostitute had a son, and one son died in the night. The woman whose son died stole the other baby in the night. Both mothers insisted they were the baby's mother. The king had an amazing solution that revealed the true birth mother. Read how he solved the problem by demonstrating Godly wisdom, identifying the true mother and thereby rendering justice for the child and the real mother.

> *Now two women who were harlots came to the king, and stood before him. And one woman said, 'O my lord, this woman and I dwell in the same house; and I gave birth while she was in the house. Then it happened, the third day after I had given birth, that this woman also gave birth. And we were together; no one was with us in the house, except the two of us in the house. And this woman's son died in the night, because she lay on him. So she arose in the middle of the night and took my son from my side, while your maidservant slept, and laid him in her bosom, and laid her dead child in my bosom. And when I rose in the morning to nurse my son, there he was, dead. But when I had examined him in the morning, indeed, he was not my son whom I had borne'. Then the other woman said, 'No! But the living one is my son, and the dead one is your son.' And the first woman said, 'No! But the dead one is your son, and the living one is my son.' Thus they spoke before the king.*
>
> *And the king said, The one says, 'This is my son, who lives, and your son is the dead one'; and the other says, 'No! But your son is the dead one, and my son is the living one.'*
>
> *[Do you see what is going on here? It is the "He said, she said" game, only in this case it is the "she said, she said."]*
>
> *Then the king said, 'Bring me a sword.' So they brought a sword before the king. And the king said, 'Divide the living child in two, and give half to one, and half to the other.'*
>
> *[Well, that is one solution, but is it a Godly solution?]*
>
> *Then the woman whose son was living spoke to the king, for she yearned with compassion for her son; and she said, 'O my lord, give her the living child, and by no means kill him!' But the other said, 'Let him be neither mine nor yours, but divide him.' So the king answered and said, 'Give the first woman the living child, and by no means kill him; she is his mother.' And all Israel heard of the judgment which the king had rendered; and they feared the king, for they saw that the wisdom of God was in him to administer justice (I Kings 3:16-28 NKJV).*

In this story, you can see how God worked through a person to administer justice on behalf of two single mothers.

But wait! There is even more! In the New Testament, in Acts 6, the Lord established a special food program so the widows would be fed. He even set up dedicated men to administer this program. How special is that?

> *But as the believers rapidly multiplied, there were rumblings of discontent. The Greek-speaking believers complained about the Hebrew-speaking believers, saying that their widows were being discriminated against in the daily distribution of food. So the Twelve called a meeting of all the believers. They said, 'We apostles should spend our time teaching the word of God, not running a food program. And so, brothers, select seven men who are well respected and are full of the Spirit and wisdom. We will give them this responsibility. Then we apostles can spend our time in prayer and teaching the word' (Acts 6:1–4 NLT).*

Today many churches have food banks which are the contemporary equivalent to the program described above. Do not forget God in the equation of your daily life. I cannot stress this enough. As you commit yourself to Him, He helps you and your children in the most unexpected ways.

> *The unfortunate commits himself to You; You have been the helper of the orphan (Psalm 10:14(b) NASB).*

Sometimes, it is hard to comprehend, yet you and your children are so close to His heart, that He even takes note of those who come against you and brings or allows consequences against them on your behalf for the way they have treated you.

You may not see the consequences, but He will accomplish His purposes nevertheless. It is not up to you to worry about *how* God brings consequences upon that other person. He may (or may not) allow you to see those repercussions in the future. That is not your business. Your responsibility is to ask the Lord for a humble heart, and pray for your "ex."

David prayed:

> *LORD, You have heard the desire of the humble; You will prepare their heart; You will cause Your ear to hear, To do justice to the fatherless and the oppressed, That the man of the earth may oppress no more (Psalm 10:17-18 NKJV).*

Speaking about God, David also says:

> *The LORD watches over the strangers; He relieves the fatherless and widow; But the way of the wicked He turns upside down (Psalm 146:9 NKJV).*

> *But you do see the trouble and grief they cause. You take note of it and punish them. The helpless put their trust in you. You defend the orphan (Psalm 10:14 NLT).*

What always astonishes me is that as you seek God, He says He will even use ungodly people to come to your rescue. This may even include your "ex" as He did for me in the following example.

> **PERSONAL EXAMPLE:** After my divorce, I had a leading by the Lord to move out of state, but the court papers had restricted my ex-husband and me from doing so without the permission of the other one. I was fearful he would not sign the release needed, but I was confident the Lord wanted us to move. I prayed for several months and then presented him with the fact I wanted to move with the children and why. To my amazement, he signed the papers without a single objection. I believe that because I humbled myself, God softened his heart to fulfill the last sentence in Psalm 68:5 KJV *"A defender of widows, is God in His holy habitation."*

Single Mom??? What Now???

CHAPTER 2

Spiritual Perspectives

FAITH: IN WHAT OR WHO?

> *So faith comes from hearing, that is, hearing the Good News about Christ (Romans 10:17 NLT).*

We all have faith in something. It is not *what* you have faith in that is ultimately important; it is *who* you have faith in.

As you go through this journey as a single mother, you will be stretched in your faith like never before. God knows this, and He has told us in advance that He is the "I AM" for all situations.

> *Moreover He said, 'I [am] the God of your father—the God of Abraham, the God of Isaac, and the God of Jacob.' And Moses hid his face, for he was afraid to look upon God (Exodus 3:6 NJKV).*
>
> *God replied to Moses, 'I AM WHO I AM. Say this to the people of Israel: I AM has sent me to you' (Exodus 3:14 NJKV).*

To me that meant He was unlimited in how He could reveal Himself to me. In addition, the phrase "I AM" indicated to me that it was present tense, something I could ask for NOW. When I read these verses, I took Him at His Word. As I discovered different names in the Bible that describe God and His nature, when I had a need, I filled it in. I AM _____.

When I wanted comfort, I prayed that He would become "I AM *your father/daddy*."

If my children were sick, I would pray that He would become "I AM *your healer*."

If I needed food, I would remind God that He said He was "*my Provider*."

You do not have to ask for spiritual needs exclusively either. At times I would not really know what I needed. Therefore, rather than trying to figure it out on my own, I would just ask God to be my "I AM."

This is not meant to be disrespectful, but once I needed my car fixed and did not know a mechanic. I was so overwhelmed I did not even know who to ask for help. Then I prayed for Him to show me how to go about finding a reliable mechanic. Soon, He fulfilled "I AM *your mechanic*" by revealing to me where to go.

He knows me best, and He knows what I need. Being comforted by this knowledge, I would pray for His nature to be revealed in my life in some tangible way to meet my needs, and He would.

There are no limits to what He will do for you; however, you have to *ask* and *expect* Him to answer. He does not want to be the last resort; He wants to be your first choice.

The following story in Luke 7 is about a single mother who experienced a double tragedy. Not only was she a widow, but her son had died too. Read how Jesus reacted when he saw her.

> *Now it happened, the day after, that He went into a city called Nain; and many of His disciples went with Him, and a large crowd. And when He came near the gate of the city, behold, a dead man was being carried out, the only son of his mother; and she was a widow. And a large crowd from the city was with her.*
>
> *When the Lord saw her, He had compassion on her and said to her, 'Do not weep.' Then He came and touched the open coffin, and those who carried him stood still. And He said, 'Young man, I say to you, arise.' So he who was dead sat up and began to speak. And He presented him to his mother. Then fear came upon all, and they glorified God, saying, 'A great prophet has risen up among us'; and, 'God has visited His people' (Luke 7:11-16 NKJV).*

The verses above are a great example of Jesus demonstrating the truth of his name, I AM. He became the "I AM the resurrection and the life" to her at that moment.

> *Jesus said to her, 'I am the resurrection and the life. He who believes in Me, though he may die, he shall live...' (John 11:25 NKJV).*

As the great "I AM," He can do anything. He is not the great Santa Claus in the sky, but nothing is impossible with Him. We just need to believe in faith that He is, that He hears us, and that He will reward us according to His will.

> *And it is impossible to please God without faith. Anyone who wants to come to him must believe that God exists and that he rewards those who sincerely seek him (Hebrews 11:6 NLT).*

I was raised to believe God existed, and I attended church faithfully. Despite this, I was a young adult before I realized God wanted to reward me with good things. I knew He had rewards for me when I got to heaven, though I did not realize He had many things He wanted to *do* for me and *be* for me while I was making my journey through life.

A single mom has had at least one hurtful relationship with a man leaving her in her present situation. This makes it hard to trust in an individual man or men in general. However, God, as your husband, will be your "I AM." The deeper the hurt, the harder it is to grasp this and trust. In spite of your pain, you need to start at point zero in your relationship with Christ. Recall how you as a single mother have trusted Him to date, and build your faith this way. Recall what Christ has already done. Then your faith can grasp "I AM" better as you recall your personal track record with the Lord. Only God can be your complete "I AM."

No one person can ever fulfill the needs of another person 100 percent of the time. This causes a false expectation and is a terrible burden to put on someone. Often a Christian woman thinks if she just had a Christian husband, all would be wonderful. This is simply not true. No partner will fulfill you, even if he is a Christian.

You cannot see the future, and you do not know whether you will ever marry or remarry, only God knows. Regardless of whether or not you have that desire, one way to prepare yourself in the interim so you are not blindsided would be to make a list of the qualities you want in a Godly spouse, referring to the Word as your guide. If someone comes along, then you will be prepared. If not, you will see by your list, areas where the Lord wants you and your child to grow. Either way, you are preparing yourself for the future God has in store for you.

To make your list, first divide it into three columns with Needs, Wants, and Desires as the headings. Needs are nonnegotiable. Wants are things you would like but could live without, and Desires are the least important, like something you wish for or crave. Add to it as you see yourself change, as your children grow, or as you discover another quality you want in a potential spouse. This is not a static list. As you grow in the Lord, the characteristics you desire will change. Refer to it periodically. That way, if and when someone comes into your life as a potential mate, you can refer to your list. Does he fit the qualities you want in a husband? If not, why not? Consider the qualities you want in a potential mate as it pertains to what you want for your child, not just yourself. You may see God's will unfold before your very eyes, just by comparing the person with your list, helping you make His choice for you more apparent to you.

The best time to do this is prior to becoming involved in a relationship. Once you are emotionally involved, or "in love," the adrenalin in our bodies produces different moods and emotions, and we are on a false high. This is why first love (and second love and third love) is so blinding. Make your list before the person even shows up in your life. If you wait until you are involved, you will subconsciously adjust the list to fit the person you are attracted to instead of letting God bring you the person that fits your list. This is a good tool, even if you never intend to get married.

If you have a daughter, you can pass this tool on to her to help her not make the same mistakes you did. You will be giving her an edge on life and marriage, probably one you never had.

> PERSONAL EXAMPLE: I had learned a lot and changed since my first marriage, so when I was a single mother, I made a list of 21 qualities I wanted in a spouse. Some of the qualities I wanted were: a pastor, someone who was not "dull, routine and boring," a person who played guitar, spoke French, and someone who could massage my body when in pain. When a certain brother-in-the-Lord began courting me, I looked at my list, and saw that the Lord had fulfilled all but one quality in my list of 21 needs, wants and desires, and the one that was lacking (and upon re-evaluation, was not critical) was the color of his hair. Therefore, it was a confirmation to me that perhaps this person was the one I was to marry. Of course, we both sought our pastor and elders' counsel, and it was confirmed in the Word before we proceeded.

THE GOD OF SECOND CHANCES

Whether you were ever married or not, you also have a heavenly husband. The kind of heavenly husband God is and how He views a single mother was addressed earlier in Isaiah 54. Single mothers and their children are very special in God's eyes.

Most single mothers have had husbands or "exes" who shamed, abandoned, or rejected them. Their "ex" may have made them feel unwelcome or unwanted, and in the process have made their children feel that way too.

On the contrary, God is not like that. He does not look upon you and your past and make you feel shame or embarrassment. He does not make you feel like damaged goods. He has already seen your circumstances, and He is not surprised at your situation. Although hard to comprehend, He knew the choices you would make and the things that would happen to you long before you did. He knows your pain, and He wants to lift you above those circumstances that hold you down. He wants to exchange your old life for the one He has planned for you. God wants to have as personal and intimate a relationship with you as you would have with an earthly husband, only better.

Chapter 2

If this is hard for you to grasp in your heart, think of a time in the past when you had a good relationship with your "ex," when you looked forward to being with him, and wanted to spend time with him. Those are the feelings you want to reflect on, knowing that in a much larger measure, that is how God wants to be with you. He wants to accelerate those positive experiences with Him exclusively, without another man.

Your earthly husband was unfaithful, but your heavenly husband is a faithful husband. Your earthly husband did not protect you; but God is a protector of widows, orphans, and the fatherless (which includes single mothers and their children). You may be able to see where God has obviously protected you from something. Or looking back, you may be able to see how He spared you from something harmful you were not even aware of, and that is a form of protection. You cannot always be with your children, but God is always their companion, and He will protect them too. He also has a plan for their life.

> *He will feed His flock like a shepherd; He will gather the lambs with His arm, And carry them in His bosom, And gently lead those who are with young (Isaiah 40:11 NKJV).*

Your earthly husband rejected and abandoned you, but as His child, God will never reject or abandon you. You can count on Him being there. Sometimes that is hard to embrace with your heart because of the hurt you have endured. At times it is hard to connect the fact that God loves you because it is hard to intellectually comprehend. It is a matter of experiencing it in your heart, not just your mind.

Regardless of one's past or present circumstances, no one is perfect and never will be. God knows that, and it does not surprise Him. He does not expect perfection. That is why He sent Jesus to die as a substitute for you. Jesus was the only perfect human being to live on earth, which is why He is the only one God could accept as payment for your sins. As a result, you have to receive Jesus in your heart in order to receive God's forgiveness. It is because of Jesus that God can forgive you and give you a second chance, a third chance, and a fourth chance, ad infinitum. He loves you just where you are, but He loves you too much to leave you the way you are. He never gives up on you even if you have given up on yourself.

The following story of Bathsheba is an excellent example of God's mercy in not only giving her a second chance, but by tremendously blessing her too. He did not just nullify what had happened to her so she did not reap the consequences; on the contrary. He had compassion on her and added great physical and spiritual riches to her. While married, she became pregnant by another man, and since he was the King of Israel, he took advantage of his position and seduced her. Then he arranged for her husband to be killed "accidentally" through a third party. All of this was to cover his sin with Bathsheba. Then after she married him and gave birth, that child died.

She had a rough time that was primarily a result of someone else's choices. Perhaps you can legitimately say some things in your life that you experienced were truly the result of someone else's bad choices. Yet, God had a plan for Bathsheba, and He has a plan for you. Her story begins in Samuel 11.

> *Then it happened one evening that David arose from his bed and walked on the roof of the king's house. And from the roof he saw a woman bathing, and the woman was very beautiful to behold. So David sent and inquired about the woman. And someone said, 'Is this not Bathsheba, the daughter of Eliam, the wife of Uriah the Hittite?' Then David sent messengers, and took her; and she came to him, and he lay with her, for she was cleansed from her impurity; and she returned to her house. And the woman conceived; so she sent and told David, and said, 'I am with child.' Then David sent to Joab, saying, 'Send me Uriah the Hittite.' And Joab sent Uriah to David. When Uriah had come to him, David asked how Joab was doing, and how the people were doing, and how the war prospered. And David said to Uriah, 'Go down to your house and wash your feet.' So Uriah departed from the king's house, and a gift of food from the king followed him. But Uriah slept at the door of the king's house with all the servants of his lord, and did not go down to his house. So when they told David, saying, 'Uriah did not go down to his house,' David said to Uriah, 'Did you not come from a journey? Why did you not go*

> *down to your house?' And Uriah said to David, 'The ark and Israel and Judah are dwelling in tents, and my lord Joab and the servants of my lord are encamped in the open fields. Shall I then go to my house to eat and drink, and to lie with my wife? As you live, and as your soul lives, I will not do this thing.' Then David said to Uriah, 'Wait here today also, and tomorrow I will let you depart.' So Uriah remained in Jerusalem that day and the next.*
>
> *Now when David called him, he ate and drank before him; and he made him drunk. And at evening he went out to lie on his bed with the servants of his lord, but he did not go down to his house. In the morning it happened that David wrote a letter to Joab and sent it by the hand of Uriah. And he wrote in the letter, saying, 'Set Uriah in the forefront of the hottest battle, and retreat from him, that he may be struck down and die.' So it was, while Joab besieged the city, that he assigned Uriah to a place where he knew there were valiant men. Then the men of the city came out and fought with Joab. And some of the people of the servants of David fell; and Uriah the Hittite died also.*
>
> *Then Joab sent and told David all the things concerning the war.... And the messenger said to David, '...your servant Uriah the Hittite is dead also.' When the wife of Uriah heard that Uriah her husband was dead, she mourned for her husband. And when her mourning was over, David sent and brought her to his house, and she became his wife and bore him a son. But the thing that David had done displeased the Lord (II Samuel 11:2-18, 23-24, 26-27 NKJV).*

Bathsheba was pregnant by a man not her husband, and then that man arranged to have her husband killed by a third party. Now, as if her circumstances were not bad enough—after she had given birth, on top of all that she had gone through, her child died. We catch up with her story about her son in Chapter 12.

So David said to Nathan, 'I have sinned against the LORD.' And Nathan said to David, 'The LORD also has put away your sin; you shall not die. However, because by this deed you have given great occasion to the enemies of the LORD to blaspheme, the child also [who is] born to you shall surely die' (II Samuel 12:13-14 NKJV).

Bathsheba could legitimately say there were lots of bad choices made all around her by others, and she reaped the consequences. I am not saying she did not have some choices; however, some consequences she reaped were not the direct result of her choices. Yet, God had another plan for her, for King David, and for Israel that no one could envision. He gave her another son, and not just any son, but a son who would become the wisest man in the world.

> *Then David comforted Bathsheba his wife, and went in to her and lay with her. So she bore a son, and he called his name Solomon (II Samuel 12:24(a) NKJV).*
>
> *Thus Solomon's wisdom excelled the wisdom of all the men of the East and all the wisdom of Egypt. For he was wiser than all men...and his fame was in all the surrounding nations (I Kings 4:30-31 NKJV).*

Bathsheba could not see God's plan ahead of time and neither can we. She could have fallen into the mindset of being a victim. Whether we are in the middle of a pit we dug ourselves, or whether it is a result of someone else's choices, we do not see the whole picture.

Bathsheba probably struggled with self-worth among other things. She must have had a lot of questions. She probably asked God, "Why me?" I do not know about you, but especially when I have reaped the consequences of another person's sin, there have been many times when I have asked God, "Why me?" However, the God who gives all of us second chances, gave her a second chance, a second child, Solomon, who eventually became King over Israel. After all she had been through, although she did not know it at the time, she was granted a great honor as well, lineage in the line of Christ.

No matter where you are today, emotionally or spiritually, divorced, never married, remarried, whatever your circumstances, God still holds out His hand to you. You are never so far removed from God's hand that He cannot touch you by changing your heart and plucking you out of your situation. He is ready to give you another opportunity by exchanging your life and all the choices you have made up to now, with His will for your life. All you have to do is receive His mercy by surrendering your will to His. If you will give Jesus your heart, you will receive another opportunity to turn your life around, and it will be more rewarding than you ever expected it would be.

Single Mom??? What Now???

CHAPTER 3

Trials and Tribulations

FORGIVING YOUR "EX"

Forgiving your "ex" is one of the hardest things to do—still it has to be done whether you ever reconcile or not. Forgiveness is imperative for you and your children to be able to continue to grow, go forward without baggage, and establish other healthy relationships. If you do not forgive your "ex" and yourself, that baggage will carry into other relationships in general and especially any relationships you may have with the opposite sex.

You need to forgive yourself as well. If you do not forgive yourself, you are saying that your opinion of yourself is higher than God's view of you. Your pride has blinded you. You are now on the throne of your life and have placed yourself higher than God.

However, you cannot truly forgive yourself or anyone else until you have been forgiven by the only person who can totally forgive you, which is God. If you have asked for forgiveness, the God of the Universe has forgiven you. How much better can that be?

Once you receive God's forgiveness, you will realize how much He wants a relationship with you, and you will see how much you fall short; in fact, we all do. That is when you will see yourself as you truly are, one who is not perfect, yet amazingly, forgiven by the One-Who-Is-Perfect. This will no longer be something you have heard about or comprehend intellectually. Once you receive His forgiveness, you will be washed clean, and you will feel a burden lifted. You will experience how much He treasures you. Then you will be in a place to truly forgive others from a pure heart completely and fully.

Forgiveness is for everyone's benefit. It was created by God to free you from feelings that are detrimental to you and to free God to be able to work in that other person's life. If you continue to hang on to unforgiveness, you are still tied to that other person, and they are still on *your* hook. On the contrary, once you forgive them, you release them from your hook. That puts them on God's hook where He can deal more effectively with them.

Chapter 3

If you think you have forgiven your "ex," then you need to do a heart check. What feelings arise when you think about him or her? Are you still angry or hurt? Then you have not forgiven your "ex."

Ask yourself: Do you want the best for them? After all, they were also created in the image of God, and He still loves them just as they are too. Can you pray a prayer of blessing towards them? If so, you have probably forgiven them for what they did or did not do.

Then again, what about the next time a contact happens: a phone call, email, text, a face-to-face meeting, or even an off-handed comment by a third party? Does just the mention of their name cause negative feelings to rise up again? Then, you need to ask yourself, "Where do those feelings come from?" Are they a result of the past and you have not truly forgiven; or is it possible the contact has initiated a *new* clash of the minds? This is a hard thing to look at. Regardless, it is for your own good and the good of your children that you examine those feelings.

If the controversy is a new conflict, then you need to forgive again for that specific reaction regarding that *current* disagreement.

In other words, let us say you have forgiven your "ex" for leaving you holding the bag. Then one day you get a phone call. It is your "ex" and he wants to exercise his right of visitation, but his idea of coming over on his time frame does not fit with yours since your child has an activity where they are previously committed. Consequently, an argument ensues. If you have truly forgiven him, it really is not any more about the fact that he left you and everything that entails. Instead, it is now currently about the fact that his visitation request is not convenient with your family's schedule. Therefore, you need to repent of your current negative reactions, and forgive him for his current behavior, AGAIN. Yes, I know that is difficult, but that is how we grow more into the image of Christ.

In fact, as long as your children are minors, and perhaps even longer, you may have many opportunities where there is a variance of opinion causing discord. One example might be the daughter who wants her natural dad to give her away at her wedding, or perhaps the son who wants to tap his dad for money for his first car. Do not confuse these new situations where you react inappropriately to mean you have not forgiven your "ex." If you truly have forgiven him and can bless him, then the act you need to repent of and forgive again is a *current* one, not one of the past. There is a difference between *initial* forgiveness for things in the past versus forgiveness for the *new* issues that crop up from time to time just because your relationship continues as a result of the link with the children.

You may be tempted to take matters in your own hands, to retaliate in some way. That is a typical human reaction; then again, you do not have to act upon it. Remember, God will take care of any unsettled scores.

> *Dear friends, never avenge yourselves. Leave that to God. For it is written, 'I will take vengeance; I will repay those who deserve it,' says the Lord (Romans 12:19 NLT).*

There is a great story about Tamar, a single woman who was raped, conceived twins through incest, was unjustly accused, and who could have taken revenge into her own hands. Instead she worked within the laws of the land which God had set up for the Israelites to receive justice. As a result, her honor was restored within her family and community. Let us look at her story in Genesis 38:6-30.

> *Then Judah took a wife for Er his firstborn, and her name was Tamar. But Er, Judah's firstborn, was wicked in the sight of the Lord, and the Lord killed him. And Judah said to Onan, 'Go in to your brother's wife and marry her, and raise up an heir to your brother.' But Onan knew that the heir would not be his; and it came to pass, when he went in to his brother's wife, that he emitted on the ground, lest he should give an heir to his brother. And the thing which he did displeased the Lord; therefore He killed him also (Genesis 38:6-10 NKJV).*

Under Israel's law, God sought to preserve families in this way. If a man married a woman and died before they had any children, then it was his brother's obligation to take that woman as his wife. As a result, the first son that was born would be named after the dead brother, and the family's name would continue in Israel.[10] The story continues:

> Then Judah said to Tamar his daughter-in-law, 'Remain a widow in your father's house till my son Shelah is grown.' For he said, 'Lest he also die like his brothers.' And Tamar went and dwelt in her father's house. Now in the process of time the daughter of Shua, Judah's wife, died; and Judah was comforted, and went up to his sheepshearers at Timnah, he and his friend Hirah the Adullamite. And it was told Tamar, saying, 'Look, your father-in-law is going up to Timnah to shear his sheep.' So she took off her widow's garments, covered herself with a veil and wrapped herself, and sat in an open place which was on the way to Timnah; for she saw that Shelah was grown, and she was not given to him as a wife (Genesis 38:11-14 NKJV).

Long after Shelah was old enough to get married, his father, Judah, had not come through with the promise of giving his third son to Tamar as the law had provided. This law was given by God to perpetuate the family name and lineage. Tamar knew this and took things into her own hands. This is a case where Tamar was looking for justice since Judah was in the wrong for withholding his son Shelah from marrying her. The story continues with Tamar by the side of the road where she knew Judah had to pass by.

> When Judah saw her, he thought she was a harlot, because she had covered her face. Then he turned to her by the way, and said, 'Please let me come in to you'; for he did not know that she was his daughter-in-law. So she said, 'What will you give me, that you may come in to me?' And he said, 'I will send a young goat from the flock.' So she said, 'Will you give me a pledge till you send it?' Then he said, 'What pledge shall I give you?' So she said, 'Your signet and cord, and your staff that is in your hand.' Then he gave them to her, and went in to her, and she conceived by him. So she arose and went away, and laid aside her veil and put on the garments of her widowhood. And Judah sent the young goat by the hand of his friend the Adullamite, to receive his pledge from the woman's hand, but he did not find her. Then he asked the men of that

> *place, saying, 'Where is the harlot who was openly by the roadside?' And they said, 'There was no harlot in this place.' So he returned to Judah and said, 'I cannot find her. Also, the men of the place said there was no harlot in this place.' Then Judah said, 'Let her take them for herself, lest we be shamed; for I sent this young goat and you have not found her.'*
>
> *And it came to pass, about three months after, that Judah was told, saying, 'Tamar your daughter-in-law has played the harlot; furthermore she is with child by harlotry.' So Judah said, 'Bring her out and let her be burned!' When she was brought out, she sent to her father-in-law, saying, 'By the man to whom these belong, I am with child.' And she said, 'Please determine whose these are—the signet and cord, and staff.' So Judah acknowledged them and said, 'She has been more righteous than I, because I did not give her to Shelah my son.' And he never knew her again. Now it came to pass, at the time for giving birth, that behold, twins were in her womb. And so it was, when she was giving birth, that the one put out his hand; and the midwife took a scarlet thread and bound it on his hand, saying, 'This one came out first.'*
>
> *Then it happened, as he drew back his hand, that his brother came out unexpectedly; and she said, 'How did you break through? This breach be upon you!' Therefore his name was called Perez. Afterward his brother came out who had the scarlet thread on his hand. And his name was called Zerah (Genesis 38:15-30 NKJV).*

The amazing thing about this story is despite Judah's sin of omission and Tamar's sin of deception resulting in assertiveness to take things into her own hands, her son Perez, became a part of the lineage of King David and part of the line of the genealogy of Jesus Christ.

Consequently, we see God is always in the business of restoring us, no matter what our past is. He still can bring good things out of bad circumstances.

Perhaps you can relate to some of Tamar's story, and how she must have felt during those nine months of pregnancy. She probably felt like an outcast among her own family, and it did not stop with the birth of her twin boys. As she raised them, probably alone, she must have continued to feel a stigma in her community.

Whatever part you can identify with, remember God is the same yesterday, today, and forever. He can restore you too. He can give you back the years the locusts have eaten. He promises:

> 'So I will restore to you the years that the swarming locust has eaten, the crawling locust, the consuming locust, and the chewing locust, My great army which I sent among you' (Joel 2:25 NKJV).

Those "locusts" might not just be about restoring a marriage. They could apply to restoring any strained relationship, that house you may have lost, or bills that became too much for you to handle. God is in the business of restoration. Stand back and let Him do His work.

SELF-WORTH/SELF-IMAGE

Just going through a divorce or separation will cause you to question your sense of self-*worth* and your self-*image*.

God gives us our self-*worth* because we are created in His image which is not based on anything we do. Only Christ can give a person the self-*worth* they deeply desire since He is the only one who sees you as you truly are and who knows all the facts about you. The great thing is, despite how you look at yourself, He looks at you differently. He knows you and your circumstances, and He is still there to encourage you. There is no one else that can consistently fulfill your needs apart from Jesus.

Although our self-*image* could be fairly accurate if it is based on how God views us, usually it is not. None of us are perfect, so we view ourselves in a distorted manner.

Our self-*image* comes from how we view ourselves based on what we do, what others have told us all our lives, and how we view our circumstances. Ultimately, this causes us to believe certain things about ourselves, both true and false. We all have mental tapes that we listen to called "self-talk." These tapes help form our self-*image*, either detrimentally or positively. These thoughts can be true, or they can be lies. We can think of ourselves as "less than" or "more than," depending on what we believe about ourselves. Remember, Satan is a liar, and negative thoughts that form, originate from him, even if they start with an "I." Some common examples are: *I* am not worthy, *I* am no good, *I* deserve to be punished, *I* can never change, etc. This is a trick from Satan making us think those thoughts originate with us. Satan has twisted them to sound like they are from us, even though they really are from him. Our minds are Satan's playground.

Sad to say though, most people do not look at themselves the way God does. Instead, they seek a tangible love relationship for the wrong reasons, hoping to fill that void that only Jesus can fill. Thinking any earthly relationship will complete you is a dangerous pattern, and single mothers are extremely vulnerable, no matter how strong or assertive they seem on the outside.

If a woman seeks love out of the wrong motivation, she may become a single mother before she marries. True love seeks to give to a relationship, not just see what one can get out of that relationship. Sadly, many times a woman desires to have a child as a status symbol. This is very detrimental to the child and has long-range consequences.

Usually a single mother has been torn down or beaten up mentally or physically by others. This may have been by one person or various men in her life; therefore, she has a harder time exerting confidence in herself or trusting men. This makes her more vulnerable and a good target for the lie of poor self-*worth*. Satan wants to rob a single mother of any confidence she might have. Satan is not out to give you a bad hair day. He is out to bring you down totally—to steal, kill, and destroy you completely.

> *[Jesus said]* '*The thief's purpose is to steal and kill and destroy. My purpose is to give them a rich and satisfying life*' *(John 10:10 NLT).*

He starts with lies—lies about ourselves and lies about others. We believe those lies, and then we begin to look at ourselves differently. We begin to believe we have poor self-*worth* and develop a poor self-*image*. Then we believe more lies, and finally, we no longer see or believe the truth about who we really are and how God looks at us.

When a single parent has poor self-*worth*, they pass that on to their children. You cannot give away what you do not have. Most young children try to push the boundaries a parent sets. For that reason, if you do not discover who you are in Christ *before* your child hits puberty, you will be rocked to the depths of your soul when their hormones start to kick in. They begin to question *their own* self-worth. They want to know: Who am I? Why am I here? The child begins to challenge authority, and anything else which is good that you or others want to instill in them. If you do not have confidence in who *you* are in Christ, then your insecurity causes doubts that open up the potential to become a stronghold for you, and that stronghold may be passed on to your child. A stronghold is like a fortress that requires defending. In this case, a stronghold is a mental way of protecting yourself, resulting in excuses that really are lies intended to defend how you think or feel about yourself. When this bad thought pattern has been in your life so long, it has a "strong" "hold" on you and needs to be resolved with God's truth. If you do not replace those negative thoughts with the positive truth of what God says, your child may develop that same pattern of thinking.

Some other signs of poor self-*worth* or poor self-*image* could be lack of personal hygiene, an unkempt home, neglected children, promiscuity, and other addictions. Poor self-*worth* can also show up as an inability to make decisions for yourself by seeking a passive route of letting others always make decisions. This is because a person does not trust what they think to be correct.

Somewhere along the line, hopefully sooner than later, you must come to the realization that you are the *parent*, not your child's friend. As a parent, you will need to learn to draw boundaries so you do not become an enabler. This will empower you in other areas of your life too.

God's heart breaks when He sees you cry. I like to think that crying is your heart leaking. Did you know He is so personal that He keeps track of all your tears and puts them in a bottle?

> *You keep track of all my sorrows (or my wanderings). You have collected all my tears in your bottle. You have recorded each one in your book (Psalm 56:8 NLT).*

If that is not enough to build up your self-*worth* and the way you look at yourself, consider this:

> *'See, I [God] have engraved you on the palms of my hands; your walls are ever before me' (Isaiah 49:16 NIV).*

God wants you to be His for all of eternity, so once you accept His Son, He engraves you on his hands. Think about that. Engraving is permanent. It means you will always be with Him. When you consider these are the same hands that were driven through with nails when He was crucified on the cross and died, it is hard not to believe that Jesus loves you.

Have you ever done something that you believed was right, but the consequences were not what you expected? This can make you feel deflated and cause you to question your self-*worth*. In the following story in Genesis 16, that is exactly what happened to Hagar.

Hagar became a single mother because she was a servant who did not have a lot of choices. She wrestled with poor self-worth after she followed the advice of her master's wife and obeyed her, and then that woman turned on her in jealousy.

> *Now Sarai, Abram's wife, had borne him no children. But she had an Egyptian maidservant named Hagar; so she said to Abram, 'The LORD has kept me from having children. Go, sleep with my maidservant; perhaps I can build a family through her.' Abram agreed to what Sarai said. So after Abram had been living in Canaan ten years, Sarai his wife took her Egyptian maidservant Hagar and gave her to her husband to be his wife. He slept with Hagar, and she conceived. When she **[Hagar]** knew she was pregnant, she **[Hagar]** began to despise her mistress **[Sarai]**. Then Sarai said to Abram, 'You are responsible for the wrong I am suffering. I put my servant in your arms, and now that she knows she is*

pregnant, she despises me. May the LORD judge between you and me.' 'Your servant is in your hands,' Abram said. 'Do with her whatever you think best.' Then Sarai mistreated Hagar; so she fled from her.

The angel of the LORD found Hagar near a spring in the desert; it was the spring that is beside the road to Shur. And he said, 'Hagar, servant of Sarai, where have you come from, and where are you going?' 'I'm running away from my mistress Sarai,' she answered. Then the angel of the LORD told her, 'Go back to your mistress and submit to her.' The angel added, 'I will so increase your descendants that they will be too numerous to count.' The angel of the LORD also said to her: 'You are now with child and you will have a son. You shall name him Ishmael,[11] for the LORD has heard of your misery. He will be a wild donkey of a man; his hand will be against everyone and everyone's hand against him, and he will live in hostility toward[12] all his brothers.' She gave this name to the LORD who spoke to her: 'You are the God who sees me,' for she said, 'I have now seen[13] the One who sees me.' That is why the well was called Beer Lahai Roi[14]; it is still there, between Kadesh and Bered. So Hagar bore Abram a son, and Abram gave the name Ishmael to the son she had borne. Abram was eighty-six years old when Hagar bore him Ishmael (Genesis 16:1-16 NIV).

This amazing story is all the more astounding when you realize that God knew beforehand that Hagar was going to conceive. Yet, He met her in her distress, in her isolation in the wilderness when she ran away, and gave her a promise to sustain her hopes as she returned to Sarai. Through this trial, Hagar realized God could see everything ahead of time, and yet He did not condemn her. As a result of this understanding, she called him You-Are-the-God-Who-Sees. He gave her a huge promise, one she probably did not understand, and certainly one she did not see fulfilled in her lifetime. Hagar's son, Ishmael, became the father of the Arab nations, just as God promised in verse 10 above.

Hagar's God is the same one who sees your mistakes before you do them and who can bring good out of what looks bad on the surface. Your part is to ask Him what He wants you to do before you act. Then you will receive the peace that passes all understanding regardless of the outcome.

> Then you will experience God's peace, which exceeds anything we can understand. His peace will guard your hearts and minds as you live in Christ Jesus (Philippians 4:7 NLT).

This type of peace does not come from humanly understanding a situation. It goes beyond considering the pros and cons or choices regarding a situation, and then making a decision and feeling relief. This peace surpasses all human understanding because it comes from above. It is supernatural.

SNARES AND TRAPS

Single mothers do not have the spiritual covering of a husband. This spiritual covering is a way for you and your children to be protected in various areas, and this is another reason God created the family to be husband, wife and children.

This need for a spiritual covering is doubly important since a single mom is making decisions that affect more than just herself. The day-to-day decisions often have far-reaching consequences that may not be perceived as readily as if she were married.

For the reason that a single mother does not have a husband to bounce things off of, they usually do not seek Godly counsel as often as their married counterparts. If they live exclusively with their children, there can be a tendency to isolate themselves more than if they are living with another adult. This makes them more vulnerable to temptations, deception, and snares.

A snare is something that catches a person off guard and before they know it, they are trapped into a lifestyle of sin they did not expect or want. Some of these are a result of never having been married or improperly balancing priorities. Others have to do with emotions all women have in common that can become exaggerated when you are a single mother. To be forewarned is to be forearmed. That is why we are going to talk about some common snares single mothers encounter.

Chapter 3

PRIORITIES

One of the first things to realize is that now you are totally accountable to God, not to the other parent and his desires. You are not accountable to leading the other parent to the Lord, (in reality, you never were); and the other parent is no longer accountable for the day-to-day decisions on how to raise your children.

Some single moms continue to contact the father long after he has made it clear that he is moving on. This is one of the hardest adjustments to make, and it is something I see continually repeated. I believe this contact is more about the mother wanting to keep a relationship going with the father than it being truly about decisions which need to be made jointly, such as custody, visitation, etc. Certainly, there are major decisions that need input from the other parent; however, in most cases, the custodial parent needs to learn to make the minor day-to-day decisions on their own.

A single mother's ministry first and foremost is primarily to her children, and a job or anything done within the church as a ministry, must follow in priority. She must keep her eye single and focused, and not get her job or any ministry she may be involved in mixed up with the children being No. 1. If she works outside the home, priority-wise that job is at least No. 2.

> **PERSONAL EXAMPLE:** Once when I applied for a job, the prospective employer asked me what I would do if my child became sick during the day. I told him I would leave immediately after making sure my job's duties were temporarily covered by someone else. Then they said they would not hire me. I knew immediately right there and then that was not the job for me, and I knew God would provide the right job for me which would allow me to keep those God-given priorities for my family.

As a working mother, I discovered this snare must be constantly reviewed since a job (and especially if your job is *also* your ministry) requires your quality time and usually your quantity time too. If you do not constantly keep your priorities straight, your child receives the leftovers.

Our priorities for *all* of us are:
First, our relationship to Christ;
Secondly to our family; and then
A job, a career, or a church ministry.

We all need to remember that ministry in the name of Christ does not substitute for relationship with Christ, and a single mom needs to be more finely attuned to this as she does not have a husband to help her see when she becomes imbalanced.

Statistics show that most people do remarry. Part of your responsibility is to train your children so they will have tools to make a successful marriage. If you model these priorities, your child will understand they are more important to you than your job. When they marry, they will more than likely want to follow these priorities, thereby making themselves a good marriage partner and a good parent.

> **HANDY HINT for everyone:** Remember, ministry *for* God does not equate to a relationship *with* God.

COPING

Sometimes it is such an effort just to cope, right? I found the hardest time to cope was at night. At the end of the day, it is easy to resent the children whether they are awake or not. It is easy to feel tied down, lonely, and probably bored. This was the hardest time for me to cope with myself, let alone anyone else. I had to redouble my efforts at meeting the needs of my children. This involved being creative in the evening hours where invariably we were all home together, tired, and quite often financially broke. However, by focusing on them and their needs, my needs were met in unexpected ways now that my eyes were off of myself in a positive way.

In addition, everyone needs time *alone with the Lord*. Even Jesus did. He withdrew himself from the crowds. In the same way, you need to withdraw and spend time with your Father in order to be able to give the best of yourself to your children. Build this into your routine now by starting with fifteen minutes a day. Your time with the Lord might not be in the evening, although it does need to be on a regular basis for you to begin to see the best results. Increase it gradually until you have regular private time with the Lord.

Besides time with the Lord, you need some time just for *yourself*. Plan to do things by yourself and for yourself. You can do things at home after the children are in bed, during their nap time, or you might consider a sitter just to get away for a few hours on a regular basis. If you cannot afford a sitter, get acquainted with other single moms or other couples and swap time so each of you can get away. We all need to find quiet time for ourselves so we can be restored on a daily basis.

I always felt I did not have enough time to get everything done. I battled chronic migraines. As a result, it was even harder for me to realize I needed a "time out" for myself. After my children were in bed, I was usually exhausted, but I still needed personal time to unwind and think.

Everybody will have something a little different that renews them. You do not need to feel guilty if you do something nice for yourself. Right now, take a moment and think about something you would like to do that will still your soul, something that will quiet your spirit.

Maybe you cannot get out of the house to do anything fun because you have a young one at home. One suggestion might be, after the children are in bed, lock yourself in the bathroom, light some candles, maybe put on some music, take a bubble bath, and enjoy some time for yourself. There is nothing wrong with that, and it will renew you for another day. Especially as a single mother, you have to be intentional about doing something for yourself. This will not happen on its own.

When my children were little, my most precious time of day was their nap time. I would use that time to read a book, or just go out in the backyard and sit in the sun. Your personal time can be very simple; however, it has to be something you enjoy, not another task "to do."

It might be only 10 or 15 minutes a day. It does not have to cost anything; however, it has to be something that will restore you mentally and emotionally in order for you to cope with your children better.

When you are emotionally healthy yourself, you will be able to approach your problems in a positive way instead of letting them drag you down. Then you will begin to view problems as challenges that can be overcome.

Taking care of yourself is not selfish. It is only selfish if you take care of yourself exclusively and do not consider the needs of others. If you are falling apart, you are no good to anyone else, and your children depend on you being there for them.

Children look to you for stability, consistency, and structure. When they experience those things, they become secure. You are their model. You cannot give them what they need if you are frazzled.

These are good habits to get into now. Later, if you do get married, you will find it easier to continue these habits. Believe it or not, you will probably have more time now to learn about the Lord than when you are married, so use it wisely.

STRESS

Dr. Kaoru Yamamoto[15] has done a lot of studies on both an adult's and a child's stress level. It is amazing how children interpret something as stressful. For instance, Dr. Yamamoto says a child may interpret needing glasses as evidence that they are going blind; or if a child is separated from their mother for only a few minutes in a supermarket, they may interpret that as their mother is "lost." Children simply interpret things differently than adults.

> **PERSONAL EXAMPLE:** When my son was about 3 years old, he had a sleepover with a friend down the street. When he came home, he asked me "Is my daddy a fireman?" I told him "No," but then I asked him why he would think so. He said "Because my friend's daddy is gone at night too." You can imagine my surprise. I thought I was doing a pretty good job of "covering up" the fact that his dad did not always come home after work. But my son knew he wasn't there to tuck him in and that he often came home in the morning after my son was up for the day. He interpreted the circumstances completely differently than what was really happening.

I have included two stress charts. One is for Adults and another is for Non-Adults (children). They are for you to rate your own stress and to rate your child's stress in the past year.

Although the charts are secular stress charts, they have been used as accurate guides by insurance companies and others in the health professions for years.

If you will take the time to prayerfully go through these charts, adding up the numbers, I think it not only will be revealing as to how much hidden stress you and your children are carrying, but it may help you make some wise decisions.

CHART A - STRESS CHART FOR ADULTS

To measure stress according to the Holmes and Rahe Stress Scale, the number of "Life Change Units" that apply to events in the past year of an individual's life are added, and the final score will give a rough estimate of how stress affects health. So consider what has happened to you in the past year, add up your score, and if your score concerns you, do something about it. Perhaps you can postpone a move or job change. Any change that is under your control is good until your score settles down in any one-year time frame.

Life event	Life change units
Death of a spouse	100
Divorce	73
Marital separation	65
Imprisonment	63
Death of a close family member	63
Personal injury or illness	53
Marriage	50
Dismissal from work	47
Marital reconciliation	45
Retirement	45
Change in health of family member	44
Pregnancy	40
Sexual difficulties	39
Gain a new family member	39
Business readjustment	39
Change in financial state	38
Death of a close friend	37
Change to different line of work	36
Change in frequency of arguments	35
Major mortgage	32
Foreclosure of mortgage or loan	30
Change in responsibilities at work	29
Child leaving home	29
Trouble with in-laws	29
Outstanding personal achievement	28
Spouse starts or stops work	26
Begin or end school	26
Change in living conditions	25
Revision of personal habits	24
Trouble with boss	23
Change in working hours or conditions	20
Change in residence	20
Change in schools	20
Change in recreation	19
Change in church activities	19
Change in social activities	18
Minor mortgage or loan	17
Change in sleeping habits	16
Change in number of family reunions	15
Change in eating habits	15
Vacation	13
Christmas	12
Minor violation of law	11

Score of 300+: At risk of illness.
Score of 150-299+: Risk of illness is moderate (reduced by 30% from the above risk).
Score 150-: Only has a slight risk of illness.
Since individual responses vary so greatly, your score is only a crude measure of your level of stress, but you will see better WHY you are stressed.[16]

CHART B - STRESS CHART FOR NON-ADULTS

A modified scale has also been developed for non-adults. Similar to the adult scale, stress points for life events in the past year are added and compared to the rough estimate of how stress affects health. So consider what has happened to your child in the past year. Add up the life change units, and if the score concerns you, do something about it. Perhaps you can postpone something to alleviate the stress on your child. Any change that is under your control is good until the score settles down in any one-year time frame.

Life Event	Life Change Units
Parent getting married/remarried	95
Unwed pregnancy	100
Death of parent	100
Acquiring a visible deformity	80
Divorce of parents	90
Fathering an unwed pregnancy	70
Becoming involved with drugs or alcohol	50
Jail sentence of parent for over one year	70
Marital separation of parents	69
Death of a brother or sister	68
Change in acceptance by peers	67
Pregnancy of unwed sister	64
Discovery of being an adopted child	63
Marriage of parent to stepparent	63
Death of a close friend	63
Having a visible congenital deformity	62
Serious illness requiring hospitalization	58
Failure of a grade in school	56
Not making an extracurricular activity	55
Hospitalization of a parent	55
Jail sentence of parent for over 30 days	53
Breaking up with boyfriend or girlfriend	53
Beginning to date	51
Suspension from school	50
Birth of a brother or sister	50
Increase in arguments between parents	47
Loss of job by parent	46
Outstanding personal achievement	46
Change in parent's financial status	45
Accepted at college of choice	43
Being a senior in high school	42
Hospitalization of a sibling	41
Increased absence of parent from home	38
Brother or sister leaving home	37
Addition of third adult to family	34
Becoming a full fledged member of a church	31
Decrease in arguments between parents	27
Decrease in arguments with parents	26
Mother or father beginning work	26

Score of 300+: At risk of illness.
Score of 150-299+: Risk of illness is moderate (reduced by 30% from the above risk).
Score 150-: Slight risk of illness.

Again, remember, since individual responses vary so greatly, the score is only a crude measure of the level of stress, but you will see better WHY your child may be showing signs of stress, and perhaps some stressors could be alleviated or postponed.[17]

I personally believe divorce, not death, should be rated tops in the Adult's Chart A, since divorce has so many more added factors than death, causing it to create a higher stress score. That is why I have created a chart that compares Death versus Divorce (Chart C).

All these charts may be helpful, not only initially in the separation/divorce situation, but throughout your life when faced with choices and changes. You are not the victim if you can make choices. And you always have a choice, even if it is to postpone something until a more suitable time.

CHART C
COMPARING ADULT STRESS
DEATH vs. DIVORCE

Usually most deaths of spouses do not include minor children at home, compared to divorces with minor children still at home. Therefore, even though the initial score of Divorce is 73, other conditions may apply specifically within the year of the divorce or may be a part of a lifestyle for years prior, thereby increasing the score and the stress level. Therefore, I have always believed that divorce with children in the home is worse than death. Add up the scores for the stress level you may be under. If your score concerns you, do something about it. Perhaps you can postpone something. Any change that is under your control is good until your score settles down in any one-year time frame.

Death		vs.	Divorce	
Death	100		Divorce	73
The following life events may occur in addition to death. Add them to the beginning score of 100. Some are usually not so abrupt, are often a matter of choice rather than necessity, and may be eased into. May also include:			The following life events usually occur within a few weeks or months of a divorce. Add them to the beginning score of 73. Many are forced conditions caused by another person, not so much by your choices. All are the same scores as in Stress Chart for Adults. May also include:	
Marital separation	65		Marital separation—could include "in and out syndrome," especially if children are involved or one spouse is a Christian and trying to forgive.	65
Marital reconciliation	45		Marital reconciliation—could include "in and out syndrome," especially if children are involved or one spouse is a Christian and trying to forgive.	45
Sex difficulties	39		Sex difficulties.	39
Financial change	38		Financial change.	38
Troubles with in-laws	29		Troubles with in-laws.	29
Spouse begins or ends work	26		Spouse begins or ends work.	26
Change in living conditions	25		Change in living conditions.	25
Revision of personal habits	24		Revision of personal habits	24
Change in residence	20		Change in residence.	20
Change in social activities	18		Change in social activities.	18
Change in sleeping habits	16		Change in sleeping habits	16
Change in number of family reunions	15		Change in number of family reunions.	15
Change in eating habits	15		Change in eating habits.	15
			Divorce may also conceivably include other life events such as:	
			Jail term/imprisonment	63
			Pregnancy	40
			Foreclosure	30
			A child(ren) leaving home either by rebellion or living with other parent	29
			Violation of laws	11

PERIODS/HORMONES/CYCLE OF EMOTIONS

Usually, since most single moms do not have regular male involvement, they are not as acutely aware of their periods and how their emotions are affecting them. A good idea is to keep a calendar of your periods and watch for cycles of emotions. You may be taking out your moods on your children in the way you discipline them and not even realize it.

Some single moms cannot handle certain TV programs, movies or romance novels. The love scenes and music bring back too much hurt and emotional swings. It is too close to home. As a single mom, if you are having trouble with sexual emotions, check what you are listening to or watching.

Jesus said,

> ... 'Take heed what you hear' (Mark 4:24(a) NKJV).

You could be subconsciously setting yourself up to feed those hurts and wounds. This is what the Bible calls "opposing yourself" or "in opposition."

> *And a servant of the Lord must not quarrel but be gentle to all, able to teach, patient, in humility correcting those who are in opposition, if God perhaps will grant them repentance, so that they may know the truth, and that they may come to their senses and escape the snare of the devil, having been taken captive by him to do his will (II Timothy 2:25 NKJV).*

Take time now to review what you are putting into your mind, and evaluate whether or not you are continually feeling wounded as a result of "opposing yourself."

SUICIDAL TENDENCIES/DEPRESSION

Most women are more emotional than men, and a single mother's negative emotions during the divorce process usually run more rampant over longer periods than might be true in other situations. It is common to be depressed during an initial separation or over the long-haul of a divorce. Surprisingly, even years later, memories blindside a single mother when least expected. What I call the "yo-yo" syndrome is very common. Your emotions go up and down, up and down. They come out of nowhere, when you least expect them, like a yo-yo.

During the first six months of my separation, although I read my Bible regularly, I was so consumed by my initial situation as a single mom that I was only stable when I was actually reading it and applying what I was reading. Much of that time I could not concentrate on the basics to keep my household running. This is normal at the first realization that the marriage or relationship is over.

Stress causes anyone to "short-circuit" mentally. I experienced this so much that sometimes my only prayer was "Lord hold onto me, and do not let me let go of you." Sometimes that is all a person can do. During this time in my life, at times the only scripture I could hang onto was:

> ...let your widows trust in Me (Jeremiah 49:11(b) NKJV).

If this is where you find yourself, keep praying because the Lord will never let go of you.

SOUL TIES

A soul tie is the bonding or knitting together of two souls in mind, will, and emotions. There are good, healthy soul ties, and there are bad, unhealthy soul ties. A healthy soul tie stabilizes a person, makes them feel secure and does not cause fear. Simply put, an unhealthy soul tie is formed when an emotional connection develops with anyone where you put their needs, desires, and opinions above God's will. When your emotional needs are not being met, it opens the door for an unhealthy soul tie to develop. The world may call this being an enabler or a co-dependent, but it is more than that. A soul tie is a spiritual issue.

You could have an unhealthy soul tie to someone you are or have been married to, a current or past sexual relationship, or even an emotional relationship which could include an adult child whose apron strings have not been cut. It may also be a family tie or a friend's influence that has become more important to you than God. Even a fantasy life can become a soul tie.

Beware of supplanting the absent partner with your child for your emotional needs, instead of fulfilling that need with God. This is a very subtle thing. Some indications would be sharing confidences with your child which are too sophisticated for a child to bear or letting a child sleep with you because of your lack of intimacy, etc. A child should never be expected to step into the shoes of an adult. Even telling a young boy that he is now the "man of the house" is not fair to the child. This puts too much burden on him, robs him of a piece of his childhood, and creates an emotional soul tie that is not healthy. He is *not* the head of the household, you are.

The amazing thing is that bad soul ties are not always easily recognizable, especially if you think you have put the past behind you. You will be able to identify an unhealthy soul tie when that person keeps showing up on your emotional radar. You can even be out of touch with that person for years and not realize you had an unhealthy soul tie with them that still may be hanging on and affecting you today.

A bad soul tie keeps you in a vicious cycle. It does not allow you to break free of that relationship and move forward in your life. Breaking a soul tie is like breaking a pencil in half. You cannot put it back in its original form. And why would you want to? Once you recognize how detrimental it has been to you, you will be thrilled to get rid of it.

To break a soul tie, you will need to:

- ✓ Ask God to forgive you of any sins you did to cause this soul tie;
- ✓ Receive His forgiveness;
- ✓ Renounce and repent of any vows you made, like "I will love you forever," or "I will never love anyone again." Do this out loud in Jesus' name. For example, "In Jesus' name, I now renounce and break any

ungodly soul ties formed between myself and _____ (name the person) as a result of _____ (name the sin.);"
- ✓ Forgive that person;
- ✓ Forgive yourself; and finally,
- ✓ Destroy any gifts that symbolize this relationship. This last step is a very important one. As long as you cannot bear to part with that item, you are still experiencing an emotional tie to them.
- ✓ Once you have done this, you must continue to cease to be involved in any way, even emotionally, with that person so you can remain free from that bondage.

GENERATIONAL SINS

We all know families where the parent drinks, does drugs or is abusive, and we see the child doing the same things. These are called generational sins. Generational sins are defined as repeating the sins of any of our parents and ancestors. Some examples of generational sins might be eruptions of anger your parents exhibited, manipulative tactics they used to get their way, fear they instilled in you through threats, etc. Perhaps these escalated into breaking things, foul language, physical, verbal or mental abuse. Instead of addressing their anger issues, you observed them excusing themselves saying "That is just the way I am." As a result, you now realize you have copied some of these behaviors. God wants to deliver you from any generational sins and give you peace instead. God's Word does not say, "It is OK, I forgive you since that is just the way you are." Instead, God's Word says He wants to change you from glory to glory.

While you are in the season of being a single mother, it is good to reflect on any addictive habits or generational sins you may have received from your parents or grandparents that you may be passing on to your child. There may be negative behaviors that affected your relationship with the other parent, and they are affecting your relationship with your child.

Reflect on your own heritage. What did you bring into your marriage or parenting that was a result of your parents' or grandparents' actions? You probably brought good things from your parents into your marriage and parenting style. On the other hand, as you reflect on your actions, are there any destructive habits? Perhaps you see things in yourself that you are doing that were just like your parents, things you vowed you would never do or be like. These are also generational sins.

Now is a great time to break those habits and sins. Only Jesus can give you freedom to break these off and become whole and healthy spiritually, physically, and mentally. You want to be the person God created you to be. Now that you are single, it is easier to reflect on those areas of bondage and become free from them because you do not have a mate who might feed those destructive behaviors. You are ultimately accountable to the Lord. You have the opportunity to turn a new page in your life. When you break off those generational sins, whole new areas will open up to you.

Maybe you did not know that if you are His born-again child, the Holy Spirit, who lives in you now, gives you the power to no longer remain under the *control* of sin.

> *We know that our old sinful selves were crucified with Christ so that sin might lose its power in our lives. We are no longer slaves to sin. For when we died with Christ we were set free from the power of sin (Romans 6:6-7 NLT).*

You can now access God's power through prayer so you can make different choices and not yield to those sins any longer, whether generational or not. You do this by declaring you are dead to sin, but alive in Jesus. You are now free from its power!

> *Even so consider yourselves to be dead to sin, but alive to God in Christ Jesus (Romans. 6:11 NASB).*

Your quality of life is affected by these sin issues; however, once the Holy Spirit lives within you, you have the power to break off those generational sins affecting you. This is not something to be done lightly, for you must be born again to have the spiritual authority to break them off. Here is how:

- ✓ Once you have accepted Jesus as your personal Lord and Savior, and you recognize those specific behaviors as generational sins, you have to agree that they are contrary to God's will for you and your family.
- ✓ Ask God to forgive you for your part in perpetuating them. Take your time and receive God's forgiveness, which He gives immediately.
- ✓ Admit you have been ignorant of their seriousness up until now, and declare verbally that you break their influence over you in the Name of Jesus Christ.
- ✓ Then tell Satan out loud that he has no more power over you because of the blood of Jesus, and tell him to leave.
- ✓ After you break and sever any generational sins which have affected you and possibly your family, replace them with what God has to say about them in His Word. In order to do that, you need to know the truth about what God says about you, and the only way to do that is to read His Word.
- ✓ Then spend time each day worshipping God and thanking him for delivering you from your destructive lifestyle.

Another thing to think about when considering a potential mate, is the addictive habits or generational sins they may be bringing into the relationship. Ask God to open your eyes to potential pitfalls to avoid. You do not want to bring another person in with generational baggage to pollute you and your children again. Remember, you are the primary overseer in your family, and God wants you and your family to be protected.

Single Mom??? What Now???

CHAPTER 4

Navigating the Divorce/ Separation Process

TO RECONCILE OR NOT?
– A GOOD QUESTION

I think this question of whether to reconcile or cut your losses and the dilemma it represents, will cause the single mom to be in confusion more than anything else. When you have cared about someone, trusted them, and been committed to that relationship, and they take you through the garbage pit, and then come back on their hands and knees, saying they are sorry and things will be different, there comes a time when you start to question the situation. The sad part is: *This may go on for years.* This up and down, in and out scenario makes it especially hard for others to maintain a relationship with the single mother, the other parent, and even the children. This affects you, your friends, and family. It makes your home life unsettled. In addition, I believe this will cause insecurity in children more than anything else. This is really where a single mother needs to reach out to others she can trust instead of isolate herself or put on a mask that everything is all right.

It will be up to you to discern the difference between Godly sorrow which shows the fruit of repentance, resulting in a permanent change in one's heart and behavior, versus worldly sorrow which says "I am sorry," but whose words are betrayed by one's actions. If this cycle is allowed to continue over and over again, it becomes what I call the "swinging door syndrome."

A good time frame to see if there truly is a sincere change of behavior is six months to a year. Behavior modification can occur, but it is an outward decision that does not affect the heart. Do not be in a hurry to reconcile. Time will reveal the truth and time will reveal their heart's motive.

During this time, you should not be living together, and both of you should be in personal and marital counseling.

Of course, the other person may not be willing to go to counseling, or finances may seemingly preclude this from happening. Even if the other party will not cooperate, it will benefit you to seek pastoral and/or professional counseling. If you truly cannot afford professional counseling, there are free resources available. Start by checking out resources offered through your church. They may have a network they can refer you to. Do not try to do this alone. If you have an established group you have been involved in, it is more likely you will receive the support you need. If you are not plugged in somewhere, then when a crisis hits, you will not have the support system in place that you certainly will need. This is why community is so important.

> **HANDY HINT for a bystander:** You can pray and be available for comfort and support, but remember, the single mother must ultimately make the decision. To keep allowing this "swinging door syndrome," reveals that one's self-worth is pretty much zero. That is where you can help her by building up her self-image and perhaps giving her clarity as to her circumstances. But otherwise in this type of situation, your hands are pretty much tied.

INCENTIVE TO RECONCILIATION

I have seen many separated and even divorced couples reconcile and make successful Christian marriages. With Jesus there is always that hope, so we need to look at how God views separation and divorce. Aside from the obvious practical reasons to stay married, God has a lot to say about marriage and separation.

There are occasions where it may be beneficial to assess the marriage situation by taking time out for a physical separation. Just because you are in conflict with each other, even in dire straits, that does not mean divorce or even a legal separation is necessarily the only answer. One or both spouses may desire a temporary physical separation for the express purpose of seeking the Lord without the distraction of the usual responsibilities that a marriage requires. This should be agreed upon by both parties, but you need to have predetermined boundaries and goals, with the ultimate goal being reconciliation. Although the guidelines below from Paul are given to all married couples, I think this principle applies even more strongly to those couples contemplating separation or divorce.

> *Do not deprive each other of sexual relations, unless you both agree to refrain from sexual intimacy for a limited time so you can give yourselves more completely to prayer. Afterward, you should come together again so that Satan won't be able to tempt you because of your lack of self-control (I Corinthians 7:5 NLT).*

As you can see, ideally separation should be a mutual decision where both parties agree not to be sexually intimate, and instead, take that time to seriously seek God to see if there is a potential to continue the relationship. During this time, neither party should be involved with another person, not even emotionally. If at all possible, both should be in individual counseling, not just marriage counseling. You cannot fix a marriage until each individual person becomes healthy.

I believe God allows this "grace space" as a cooling-off period within the situation so each person can see a different perspective without the other person affecting them 24 hours a day. Sometimes we do not know what we have until we have lost it.

During this time of separation, trust needs to be rebuilt. Both partners need to be virtuous in their behavior in order to win the other one over and show they are serious in their commitment.

I believe counseling is a must at this point for the reason that you need an unbiased and objective opinion to discern whether the other partner is sincere or not in his repentance. I have seen too many single mothers jump back into the marriage before the other partner has proven he has *truly* repented. As I said before, a good rule of thumb is six months to a year of observing their behavior, as well as their words, to ensure that someone has truly changed. This should be a time of not just you observing, but also others in leadership in the Body of Christ being involved enough with the other partner to be able to speak into his life. This gives you another perspective, and God often uses outside sources as a form of protection.

When you are in the separation stage and working on reconciliation, I believe the other partner should value you enough to be courting you. Old habits die hard, and it is so easy to want the conflict to end and peace to reign in your family that it is easy to overlook red flags that might be obvious to an outside observer. Let him work at winning you over again like he hopefully did at the beginning of your relationship.

Even after all avenues have been exhausted, for example, temporary separation, prayer, and counseling, God does allow permanent separation. Nevertheless, He has certain guidelines. The separated partners must remain unmarried or reconcile with each other.

> *Now to the married I [Paul] command, yet not I but the Lord: A wife is not to depart from her husband. But even if she does depart, let her remain unmarried or be reconciled to her husband. And a husband is not to divorce his wife (I Corinthians 7:10-11 NKJV).*

One definition of "reconcile" in the Greek means "to return to favor with, be reconciled to one."[18] Reconciled in this context does not necessarily mean that you remarry them or that the marriage is restored, but rather that the relationship is put back onto friendly terms and that conflict is ended.

The verses above are much easier to apply if *no* adultery is involved on the sides of either of the partners. If there is no third party muddying up the marital waters, it is more likely that reconciliation may take place or at least the separation process can be experienced with less confusion and hurt.

An obvious problem is when it is not a joint decision and one person unilaterally decides to separate. This opens the door for the other partner to more easily become involved with someone else and commit adultery. No doubt this is heartbreaking, for then the responsibility for a decision falls solely to you, the one who so desperately wants to work things out. You will need to count the cost of a separation when the other partner is not willing to work on the marriage. There may never be reconciliation or restoration of either the relationship or the marriage. If so, it will be more difficult emotionally at this stage, but it is still God's design for both of you to remain single and uninvolved with another person. By keeping yourself chaste, you will not give Satan a chance to heap guilt on you.

Yet, at times, we do have to be realistic. God does not violate a person's free will. Separation does not always work out in the ways you had hoped or even prayed for. By you serving the Lord, you are a living example that creates conviction on the part of the other party. At times that conviction pushes them further away. However, if you are seeking God and obeying Him, you do not need to carry that burden. Make God your passion, and turn your heart towards Him. He will fill that vacuum for love and the intimacy you feel is lacking. Remember, He created you for Himself, and He desires you to be fulfilled in Him alone.

I have observed that if there is *no* known adultery occurring, or none perceived, women, more than men, and especially single mothers, cling to the desire of reconciliation for the sake of the children. If this describes you, I commend you; however, please consider that the other partner may never repent. Or, if they do repent, it may be so much later that they may already have moved on emotionally and are not willing to reconcile to the point of remarriage.

Statistics indicate that your "ex" will eventually remarry or at least become involved in another relationship. If the other partner becomes involved in another sexual relationship during the separation period, that will bump the separation up to another level. Once they have broken their wedding vow, whether through remarriage or another sexual relationship, you will be scripturally free to divorce and remarry. Until that time, a great heart check to consider before permanently splitting is to ask yourself, "Am I willing to remain single the rest of my life and live a God-honoring lifestyle? What? Stay unmarried for the rest of my life? Oh my!" Well, that is what the verses above in

I Corinthians 7:10-11 indicate, which makes it a great incentive to try to work things out, especially when you have children, don't you think?

On more than one occasion I have seen the other partner repent immediately prior to a final decree being granted. When this happens, it can cause a lot of angst if your bent has been to just cut off the relationship. So the first course of action is to forgive. This needs to be done whether you plan to restore your marriage or not. Restoration means to return something to its previous condition. So before jumping back into your marriage too quickly, you need to take your time and seek the Lord as to which direction to follow—to restore your marriage or continue down the path already set in motion by a legal separation or divorce. Again, do not neglect outside Christian counsel.

God allows a scriptural divorce for adultery.

> *[Jesus said]* '*And I say to you, whoever divorces his wife, [or husband] except for sexual immorality, and marries another, commits adultery...*'

Some pastors also consider abandonment a valid reason for a divorce. The question of divorce will be more fully developed in the section entitled "Divorce." But since we are not at that stage in the process yet, let us continue to look at a possible reconciliation from the point of a *legal* separation.

When there is *no* adultery at the time of separation, or it *appears* there is no adultery, and the other partner is still not willing to do a trial separation and wants to end the relationship, if you are trying to obey God's Word about adultery being the only grounds for divorce, you may feel "trapped." Now what do you do? Let me assure you, God does not trap a person or tempt us to sin. Instead He gives us other avenues to utilize.

> *The temptations in your life are no different from what others experience. And God is faithful. He will not allow the temptation to be more than you can stand. When you are tempted, he will show you a way out so that you can endure (I Corinthians 10:13 NLT).*

If you believe you cannot scripturally divorce because adultery is not obvious, and yet you know you need to take care of your family, God gives us a legal system. There is no need to feel guilty about pursuing these legal avenues as the next step. For your children's sake, you may be forced to go to court to get spousal and/or child support, to clarify visitation rights or even obtain a restraining order. If severing the relationship permanently is not your desire, remember, you can always start the legal process for financial reasons or practical protection, but you do not need to be the one who makes the final application for divorce. It will remain in limbo until one of the parties initiates the final legal document, and that does not have to be you.

If adultery *is* involved, God does permit divorce; although, the ultimate solution is for both parties to repent of their sins, forgive each other, and reconcile. True forgiveness on the part of both parties can heal marriages. God's agapē love can overcome even the sin of adultery, the hardness of hearts, and enable you to truly forgive.

The Book of Mark reveals to us what Jesus said about this.

> *Some Pharisees came and tried to trap him with this question: 'Should a man be allowed to divorce his wife?' Jesus answered them with a question: 'What did Moses say in the law about divorce?' 'Well, he permitted it,' they replied. 'He said a man can give his wife a written notice of divorce and send her away.' But Jesus responded, 'He wrote this commandment only as a concession to your hard hearts' (Mark 10:2-5 NLT).*

Allowing God to soften your heart to forgive is taking the higher ground Jesus desires, whether your marriage is ever restored or not.

In looking at separation and divorce from an additional angle, in an age of AIDS and STDs, if your "ex" has been unfaithful, you need to ask yourself what new dynamics regarding physical issues he might be bringing home to you. You can forgive, but reconciling does not always mean you will get back together sexually. None of these decisions are easy, which is why you need to depend on God every step of the way.

Chapter 4

Up until now, I have been focusing on *you* being the wronged party. But if *you* are the one who has been unfaithful and broken your wedding vows, then you need to repent, forgive yourself, ask forgiveness from the other partner, and try to reconcile. However, if the wronged party is not willing to reconcile with you, then you are free to remarry.

I know there are those who would counsel that if you are the one who caused the divorce then you can never remarry, but divorce is not the unforgiveable sin. God will forgive you if you confess and truly repent. He would not be a just God if He forgave you of adultery, yet continued to hold it over your head in such a way as to not allow remarriage. That would be a punishment. I think the third verse of the hymn, *It Is Well with My Soul*, says it best:

> My sin, oh, the bliss of this glorious thought!
> My sin, not in part but the whole,
> is nailed to the cross, and I bear it no more,
> praise the Lord, praise the Lord, O my soul! [19]

"My sin, *not in part* but the whole"...that is what God nailed to the cross, ALL of your sin, including adultery. It seems to me that by repenting you are starting with a fresh slate and that would include the freedom to remarry. Of course, there are natural consequences of a broken home, no matter whose fault it was, and those are the challenges you will deal with the rest of your life.

I would caution you, however, not to move on to a new relationship quickly. If you do not remain single, a whole new set of dynamics appears when you start to invest in a new relationship while your child is still in the home. You are giving your time and effort to a new person, and your time with your children is now divided.

THE GRIEVING PROCESS

When a divorce or legal separation occurs, or even when a sexual relationship ends, there is a grieving process that occurs similar to when a partner dies. Often a single mother thinks she is abnormal as she begins to go through this process because she does not realize she is grieving. I cannot tell you how many people I have met who are dealing with separation or divorce and do not understand they are actually dealing with a grieving process too.

I believe that divorce creates ghosts of the past which keep surfacing if the "ex" remains in the picture. With the past haunting you, either in your mind or in reality, a single mother will relive a lot of memories and feelings longer than if the other party had died. These memories might be stirred up by another person's conversation, with phone calls, or by letters. However, with death, it is final, and you can make cleaner choices, change your lifestyle, and go on.

When a relationship is broken through separation and divorce, there is a jagged tearing, as opposed to a clean cut when a death occurs. When someone dies, it is like a clean surgical cut that heals faster, and you can move on more rapidly. On the other hand, when divorce occurs, the cut takes twice as long to heal because it is jagged and goes from side to side.

Much of the grieving that occurs in a divorce is the same as in any general grief process since there is a dying of the relationship. This grieving process can even start before the relationship actually physically or geographically ends because the process can apply to many situations leading up to a separation or divorce, such as loss of a job, economic downturn, or even a pet dying.

Years ago, the following chart detailing a general grieving process was presented in church by a grief counselor. It made a lasting impression on me, and I wanted to share it as another tool to help understand and deal with the process of grief and the direction it takes.

Chapter 4

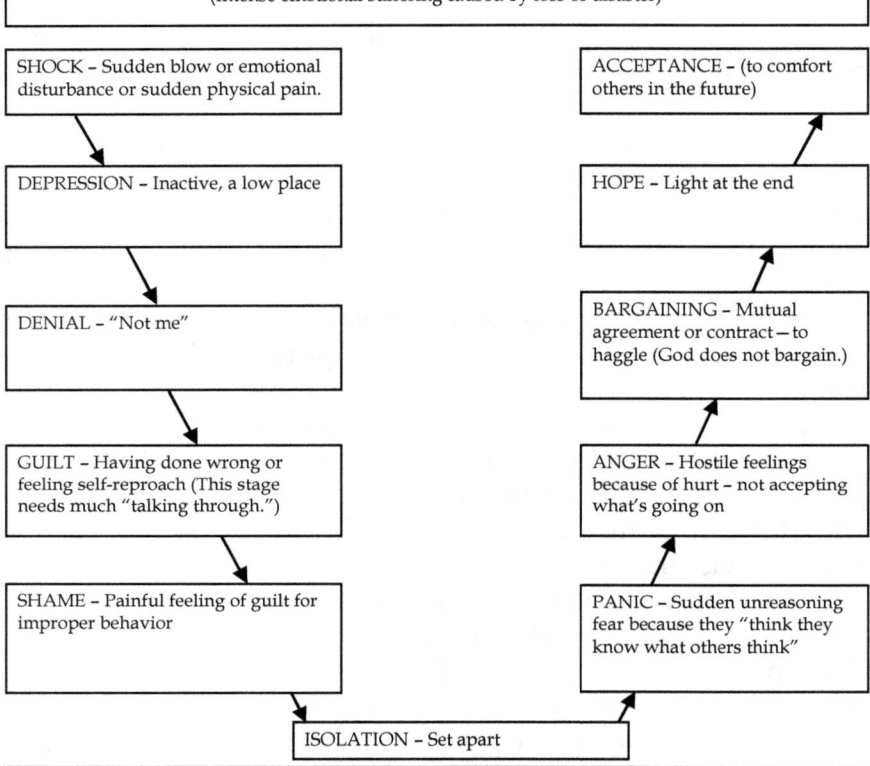

"GOOD GRIEF" PROCESS
(Intense emotional suffering caused by loss or disaster)

- SHOCK - Sudden blow or emotional disturbance or sudden physical pain.
- DEPRESSION - Inactive, a low place
- DENIAL - "Not me"
- GUILT - Having done wrong or feeling self-reproach (This stage needs much "talking through.")
- SHAME - Painful feeling of guilt for improper behavior
- ISOLATION - Set apart
- PANIC - Sudden unreasoning fear because they "think they know what others think"
- ANGER - Hostile feelings because of hurt - not accepting what's going on
- BARGAINING - Mutual agreement or contract — to haggle (God does not bargain.)
- HOPE - Light at the end
- ACCEPTANCE - (to comfort others in the future)

This "grieving" process can be triggered by any type of loss—death, divorce, loss of a relationship, house burning down, etc. You can experience these steps out of order and/or more than one at a time. All are normal and necessary. **This grieving process is a safeguard from God.**

The crux/turning point of the "Good Grief cycle" is that God becomes (is) Lord not (just) Saviour. The "Good Grief cycle" then is used to pass on to others in comfort. Recognize this cycle and get prayer support and a group to support you.

> *Most assuredly, I say to you that you will weep and lament, but the world will rejoice; and you will be sorrowful, but your sorrow will be turned into joy (John 16:20 NKJV).*

> *We know all things work together for good to those who love God, who are the called according to His purpose (Romans 8:28 KJV).*

You must constantly apply II Corinthians 10:4-5 KJV:

> *For the weapons of our warfare [are] not carnal, but mighty through God to the pulling down of strongholds; Casting down imaginations, and every high thing that exalteth itself against the knowledge of God, and bringing into captivity every thought to the obedience of Christ...*

> **HANDY HINT for those counseling a single parent:** Once a single parent realizes they are going through a process, they are more likely to cope if they are reassured they are just "normal" or "on schedule" such as described in the grief cycle. Therefore, it is a helpful thing to know the various stages a single parent may be going through.

One of the first confusing things a single mother finds herself dealing with is a *multiple* grieving process. She may not recognize it as such, but it is. There are losses she must mourn to be able to come through this time in her life so she can become healthy and whole. This process consists of more than one loss. There are different stages one goes through as well.

The grieving process from death in the Old Testament was demonstrated through many customs, and they were visible, outward signs for others to be aware of. If it was not the death of a parent, the grieving process formally lasted 30 days. If it was a parent, the grieving process was 12 months. [20] For that reason, do not try to rush this process. You will not bounce back from this stage quickly, so do not beat yourself up if you do not think you are bouncing back or moving on as rapidly as you would like to.

In addition, you need to recognize your children will be grieving too. Frequently, the single mother is in such emotional turmoil herself that she glosses over the fact or simply does not realize that her child is also going through their own grief process. Because the child has partially or totally lost a parent, divorce can feel like a form of abandonment to them. For this reason, their grieving may take longer than yours.

On the flip side though, there comes a time where you will need to move on without clinging to the drama of it all.

There are actually three grieving processes going on which may overlap from time to time.

One is for the *actual person*;

One is for the *institute of marriage* (if you were married);
One is for your *child's relationship* with the absent parent.

While going through this process, it will be helpful to try to distinguish the difference. These three stages may not strike you at the same time, and you may get over one before the other.

The first part of grieving is for the *actual person* and includes their absence from your daily life, which takes moment-by-moment adjustments. One simple example would be they no longer sit in the same spot at the dinner table, and that takes an adjustment, or you have to start mowing the lawn because they used to do that or ... (you fill in the blank). All kinds of routines will change. Realizing things like this may hit you like a ton of bricks. It is another loss, another piece of the grieving process.

In addition, grieving for the *actual person* may include the *supernatural* desire of carrying the burden of the "ex's" soul. After all, part of what any single parent has experienced in their situation, whether widowed, divorced, or never married, has probably felt like they were going through a type of hell. You may temporarily feel this way, yet, as a Christian, your desire should be that your "ex" not experience eternal hell. Prayer on their behalf is your key, your weapon to come through this aspect of grieving.

If the single mom is praying for the "ex's" repentance, and one day suddenly realizes she has not prayed for them for awhile, that is the Lord's way of removing that burden. You should not feel guilty if your concern for the other partner is not as acute as it was previously. After awhile the burden will come less often, perhaps not occurring for months or even years. This should be something God brings to mind from time to time for prayer and should not be a cause for guilt.

Another part of the grieving process for the *actual person* will be a desire brought on by lack of companionship and/or a sexual partner. Satan will attempt to tempt you in this way regarding your own physical and sexual desires over and over again to get your eyes off God. He wants to try to turn your heart into seeking your "ex" again or another person. Remember, God does not bring these things to your mind to tempt you or condemn you. You can never recapture physically being a virgin again; nonetheless, you can choose to be chaste and walk in a celibate lifestyle. God will give you the ability to walk uprightly and not feel condemned if you ask Him to give you strength to avoid temptation.

> *There is therefore now no condemnation to those who are in Christ Jesus, who do not walk according to the flesh, but according to the Spirit (Romans 8:1 NKJV).*

Secondly, if you were married, there is the grieving for the actual *institute of marriage*. Sometimes it is hard to distinguish between grieving the loss of your *marriage* and grieving the loss of the *person*. If you both made your marriage vows before God, that covenant was "until death do you part." When one of the partners walks away from that covenant, it creates a loss that was never expected.

> *'Haven't you read,' he [Jesus] replied, 'that at the beginning the Creator 'made them male and female,' and said, 'For this reason a man will leave his father and mother and be united to his wife, and the two will become one flesh'? So they are no longer two, but one. Therefore what God has joined together, let man not separate' (Matthew 19:4-6 NIV).*

In the eyes of God, that union has been *spiritually* broken, yet only a person or a court *legally* breaks that union. It takes two to make a marriage work, and if one is not willing, God does not violate a person's free will. Neither does He blame or disapprove of you. If you tried to make the marriage work to the best of your ability, then the finger pointing you might feel is not coming from God. Maybe you even followed Godly counsel, and it seemed to backfire. I can assure you those negative thoughts are coming from another source, not God.

This is one place where the guilt of failing as a partner comes into play strongly—the "If only I had done this," or "If only I had not said that." This is Satan's game, and even though this is his ploy, you do not have to dwell on these thoughts or feelings. If you realize that you are not the only one who hears these accusations in their minds, and you reject them based on God's Word, these thoughts and feelings will eventually leave as God's way of healing.

Finally, there is the grieving process of coming to the realization that the relationship is over as far as your previous role with the other partner as you have known it, but it is *not over for your children*. Remember, your children are grieving too. If you can step away from your own feelings, and tend to your child's emotional needs, you will create more stability during this season and create a closer relationship with your children than if you ignore their needs, or justify yourself by thinking they are bouncing back or doing just fine. Trust me, they are *not* doing "just fine." They are processing and interpreting what is going on, whether they verbalize it or not, and they are probably misinterpreting the situation. This is why you must get in touch with what they are thinking in order for you to be able to address the issue in a positive manner and correct any misunderstandings they may have.

Hopefully, your "ex" will still be a positive influence in your child's life, yet it may not pan out that way. You will see your child hurting, and *you* will hurt because of *their* hurt. This feeling comes and goes for an indefinite period of time. Remember that in conceiving a child you became "one flesh" with the other parent. Now you are no longer "one flesh" with them; nevertheless, your child will always be part of their flesh because of the physical union you shared.

In addition, this is a good time for me to emphasize that you should never bad-mouth the absent parent. Doing so will only backfire on you. Trying to turn a child against the other parent will only cause the child to be overcurious or want to protect the other parent from you. It may even result in your child rejecting you or lying to you about what the other parent did or said.

I have seen single parents question their child after they have been visiting the other parent. This puts the child in a defensive mode. In actuality, if the Lord wants you to know something, it will be revealed to you in a natural way, whether from the child or another source. So, do not go digging for information.

If the absent parent abandoned the child early in life or has remained out of the picture as the child is growing up, the child may imagine them in a positive light, even to the point of fantasizing about them. They usually will not verbalize this thought process, as they are not sophisticated enough to recognize what is happening and explain it to you.

However, when children become adults, they usually see both their parents for who they really are. As the saying goes, "It all comes out in the wash." Until then, you can state the truth, being careful not to add details that your child does not need to know or cannot handle.

DIVORCE

Divorce rips you apart. There is no getting around it. You cannot avoid those feelings, *even if you are the one who initiated it or wanted it.* If you have a child, its tentacles will reach out and grab you for years to come. This is just a warning, so do not be surprised. If you truly loved your "ex" and are trying to walk as a Christian, you will do a lot of soul searching before, during, and after the divorce. This can be an opportunity for great exponential spiritual growth for you.

If you are the child of divorced parents, you will probably agree with experts who say that adult children still feel the effects of trauma of their divorced parents. "Divorce may liberate parents, but it traps their sons and daughters for years."[21]

Jesus had a lot to say about divorce. Consequently, when all is said and done, you need to have a clear conscience regarding any part you played about a decision to divorce. You will need to feel confident in your decision, even if your "ex" was the one who left. Questions about that decision will come up in the future when you least expect it, often blindsiding you. That is why your conscience needs to be free from doubt when you start down the road of separation, ultimately leading to divorce.

Chapter 4

> **PERSONAL EXAMPLE:** For years, until I remarried, when I would fill out forms which would ask me to indicate if I was married, divorced or single, just contemplating making that check in the box would cause me to do a double take and admit I was a divorcee'. But I would quickly mentally run over why I was in that situation and how I got there. Then because I had followed God's guidance through the process, I'd feel a peace come over me so I could make that check mark without remorse or doubt.

You need to be able to look back on your decision, be confident in knowing God was a part of your decision, and why you made it. Then you will have the peace that Jesus speaks of which cannot be robbed from you. The following verses in Matthew 19 explain how God views divorce.

> *The Pharisees also came to Him, testing Him, and saying to Him, 'Is it lawful for a man to divorce his wife for just any reason?' And He answered and said to them, 'Have you not read that He who made them at the beginning 'made them male and female,' and said, 'For this reason a man shall leave his father and mother and be joined to his wife, and the two shall become one flesh? So then, they are no longer two but one flesh. Therefore what God has joined together, let not man separate.' They said to Him, 'Why then did Moses command to give a certificate of divorce, and to put her away?' He said to them, 'Moses, because of the hardness of your hearts, permitted you to divorce your wives, but from the beginning it was not so. And I say to you, whoever divorces his wife, except for sexual immorality, and marries another, commits adultery; and whoever marries her who is divorced commits adultery'* (Matthew 19:3-9 NKJV).

From these verses, we see God does *allow* divorce for a hard heart, though He does not like it.

> *'For I hate divorce!'* says the LORD, the God of Israel (Malachi 2:16 NLT).

Nevertheless, He does not keep a score card so you should not either. Even if you *feel* like it, you are not a second-class citizen.

You are priceless to God, even now. While you are going through a separation or divorce you probably do not *feel* valued much, if at all. In the carbon stage, before being pressurized, a diamond has little value. A diamond is just concentrated carbon, to be exact, a piece of charcoal. Perhaps right now you can relate more to the carbon stage of a diamond than to the polished diamond itself. Yet, when mined, cut, and polished, it becomes the most precious gemstone in the world. Right now you are in the pressurized stage, which is temporary and which will pass. However, in His sight, at this very moment, He sees you as being his finished, treasured diamond having much value and significance.

This is not the time to be without emotional support. You need to have someone who can keep you sane and on track, since at times you will feel like you are losing it. I do not mean someone who will agree with you and how badly you are being treated (even if it is true); instead, it needs to be someone who can objectively assess the situation from the perspectives of *both* parties. Finding someone like this may be hard, yet it is especially needed because of your children. This is not just going to affect you, it will also affect them. No person is 100 percent right all the time; but that is hard to see when you believe, and maybe rightfully so, that you are the wronged party. You need someone who is objective, and ideally someone who knows both parties, one who can speak hard, yet honest words to you without jeopardizing your friendship. Ask the Lord to open your eyes to see if He has already provided such a person in your life.

Chapter 4

PRACTICAL STAGES AND THEIR EMOTIONAL COUNTERPARTS

Have you ever asked yourself, "What did I do to deserve this?" Well, I did, many times, and then I discovered this scripture:

> *You must worship no other gods, for the LORD, whose very name is Jealous, is a God who is jealous about his relationship with you (Exodus 34:14 NLT).*

And then I asked myself, "What does that mean?" Unlike Oprah Winfrey who stopped short when she heard that God is Jealous, and then erroneously decided that if God is a Jealous God, she did not want any part of Him, I studied it a little further.

God is Jealous FOR YOU! He is not jealous *of* you, He is jealous on your behalf. He sets His affections on you and on your children so much that He is watching you all the time. If someone comes against you, mistreats you, treats you unfairly, because you are the apple of His eye, He comes with a desire to meet those negative actions with His caring nature. He feels your pain, your disappointment. He is desirous of righting that wrong and setting your path straight. However, you need to let Him into your life to receive His protection.

As you begin to start facing up to the fact that a divorce, without God's intervention, is probably inevitable, you will go through an unsettling time. Some of these stages are similar to the previous grief process which we have discussed earlier, which is more general and can apply to many situations of loss. Nonetheless, the following transitional period is more specific to separation and divorce. This particular transitional period overlaps with the *practical* stages of a divorce, but emphasizes more the *feelings* experienced during the process.

Shock and Denial

The first part of the process involves feeling *shock and denial*. You cannot believe it is true, that "it is not really happening to me." You experience *anger* and ask: "Why me?" You feel *disappointment*. You may also try *bargaining with God*. This may take the form of you wanting another chance by changing your behavior, or you may try to bargain with God about changing your "ex." Trust me, bargaining with God does not work. Do not waste your time. You will always be unsuccessful.

Loss and depression

The second set of feelings is *loss and depression*. This is probably the most difficult and may include *retreating* into your shell, *shrinking back* from relationships, *withdrawal* (even from your children), *unbelief,* and possibly *thoughts of suicide*. You will feel like you are going through or are stuck in the "valley of the shadow of death." Depression opens the door to bitterness.

Bitterness must be conquered before you can go on to another relationship and make it successful. This is one reason why people tend to remarry or become involved with the same types of people, temperament-wise, and repeat the same problems with a new person.

Therefore, I ask you: Will this trial make you *bitter* or *better*? You have a choice.

One woman who let herself become bitter was Naomi. She was a widow, possibly becoming a single mother of two boys while they were young. By the time we catch up with her in the story in Ruth 1, her sons had married and died, and she had become bitter with her circumstances.

> Now it came to pass, in the days when the judges ruled, that there was a famine in the land. And a certain man of Bethlehem, Judah, went to dwell in the country of Moab, he and his wife and his two sons. The name of the man was Elimelech, the name of his wife was Naomi, and the names of his two sons were Mahlon and Chilion—Ephrathites of Bethlehem, Judah. And they went to the country of Moab and remained there. Then Elimelech, Naomi's husband, died; and

she was left, and her two sons. Now they took wives of the women of Moab: the name of the one was Orpah, and the name of the other Ruth. And they dwelt there about ten years. Then both Mahlon and Chilion also died; so the woman survived her two sons and her husband. Then she arose with her daughters-in-law that she might return from the country of Moab, for she had heard in the country of Moab that the Lord had visited His people by giving them bread. Therefore she went out from the place where she was, and her two daughters-in-law with her; and they went on the way to return to the land of Judah. And Naomi said to her two daughters-in-law, 'Go, return each to her mother's house. The Lord deal kindly with you, as you have dealt with the dead and with me. The Lord grant that you may find rest, each in the house of her husband.' So she kissed them, and they lifted up their voices and wept. And they said to her, 'Surely we will return with you to your people.' But Naomi said, 'Turn back, my daughters; why will you go with me? Are there still sons in my womb, that they may be your husbands? Turn back, my daughters, go—for I am too old to have a husband. If I should say I have hope, if I should have a husband tonight and should also bear sons, would you wait for them till they were grown? Would you restrain yourselves from having husbands? No, my daughters; for it grieves me very much for your sakes that the hand of the Lord has gone out against me!' Then they lifted up their voices and wept again; and Orpah kissed her mother-in-law, but Ruth clung to her. And she said, 'Look, your sister-in-law has gone back to her people and to her gods; return after your sister-in-law.' But Ruth said: 'Entreat me not to leave you, Or to turn back from following after you; For wherever you go, I will go; And wherever you lodge, I will lodge; Your people shall be my people, And your God, my God. Where you die, I will die, And there will I be buried. The Lord do so to me, and more also, If anything but death parts you and me.' When she saw that she was determined to go with her, she stopped speaking to her.

Now the two of them went until they came to Bethlehem. And it happened, when they had come to Bethlehem, that all the city was excited because of them; and the women said, 'Is this Naomi?' But she said to them, 'Do not call me Naomi; call me Mara, for the Almighty has dealt very bitterly with me. I went out full, and the Lord has brought me home again empty. Why do you call me Naomi, since the Lord has testified against me, and the Almighty has afflicted me?' So Naomi returned, and Ruth the Moabitess her daughter-in-law with her, who returned from the country of Moab. Now they came to Bethlehem at the beginning of barley harvest (Ruth 1:1-22 NKJV).

In the next chapter we watch the story develop.

There was a relative of Naomi's husband, a man of great wealth, of the family of Elimelech. His name was Boaz (Ruth 2:1 NKJV).

Now, if you remember the previous story of Tamar and the law which provided a way for a family's lineage to continue through a brother, this is a similar situation. Boaz is in Naomi's deceased husband's family, and this is another way for the family's lineage to continue.[22] In view of that understanding, we pick up the story in Chapter 4.

So Boaz took Ruth and she became his wife; and when he went in to her, the LORD gave her conception, and she bore a son. Then the women said to Naomi, 'Blessed be the LORD, who has not left you this day without a close relative; and may his name be famous in Israel! And may he be to you a restorer of life and a nourisher of your old age; for your daughter-in-law, who loves you, who is better to you than seven sons, has borne him.' Then Naomi took the child and laid him on her bosom, and became a nurse to him. Also the neighbor women gave him a name, saying, 'There is a son born to Naomi.' And they called his name Obed. He is the father of Jesse, the father of David (Ruth 4:13-17 NKJV).

As Naomi went through this process, she had support from older, wiser, women who encouraged her. Finally, as a grandmother, her heart was changed, and by the end of the Book of Ruth, we see God has given her a place in the lineage of Christ. What an honor!

This is a good example of a woman who felt she had every right to be angry, so she blamed God, and let herself become bitter. If you feel like life has dealt you a bad hand, it is easy to forget that God's hand was in it, and still is, and He is working in the background to bring good out of your circumstances. Instead of dwelling on your negative circumstances, you must resist those thoughts. To fight the thought that will make you bitter, sometimes you need to take your thoughts captive minute-by-minute. You need to say NO to the negative thoughts and YES to the good things God has in store for you.

> *The weapons we fight with are not the weapons of the world. On the contrary, they have divine power to demolish strongholds. We demolish arguments and every pretension that sets itself up against the knowledge of God, and we take captive every thought to make it obedient to Christ (II Corinthians 10:4-5 NIV)*

One way of applying the principle of "taking every thought captive" that might be helpful is this: You can apply a 30-second rule to your thought life. When any thought, positive or negative, comes into your head, you have approximately 30 seconds to decide what to do with it before it goes into your heart. You can act upon it, and accept or reject it, or you can ignore it. This principle is like the truckers' expression of saying "10-4" which means, "Over and out." You will notice, the scripture reference in II Corinthians 10:4-5 is the same. This will help you remember where this principle is found when you want to recall it.

No matter which choice you make, it will still affect your heart, your emotions, and your behavior for better or worse, depending on the thought. Therefore, how much better would it be to take that thought captive immediately, and examine it to see if it lines up with God's nature and the Word. Then replace that negative thought with the following verse, which is God's desire for you instead.

> *'For I know the thoughts that I think toward you,' says the LORD, 'thoughts of peace and not of evil, to give you a future and a hope' (Jeremiah 29:11 NKJV).*

> **[He has plans for you, and they are <u>good</u>. You have a future, not suicide, not depression, not discouragement, but a future full of hope.]**

Ambivalence and anger

The third series of feelings is *ambivalence and anger* (again). Ambivalence is revealed through *acceptance*, but you are neither depressed nor angry. Although you have worked through some of the process, you are *void of feelings*. You are numb. You go through the motions of daily life; however, you feel no pain, and there is no struggle either. As the depression lifts, *anger* returns again.

All of the previously mentioned feelings cause both *loneliness* and *rebound relationships* which are very prevalent in the first stages of divorce. Loneliness causes an emotional void, often causing desperation and a vulnerability which opens you up for rebound relationships. Experts recommend waiting at least four or more years before remarrying.[23] Since experts also say blended families take six to seven years to stabilize,[24] that is a good reason to take your time, and get to know the person well to whom you are considering a future relationship.

Reorientation of Lifestyle and Identity

The next set of feelings brings questions about *reorientation of lifestyle and identity*. You ask: "Who am I?" You begin to work through who you really are, (personally, vocationally, sexually, and socially) apart from a relationship.

Building A New Life

Finally, by addressing your feelings in the process of divorce, you begin *building a new life* by putting effort into yourself in a Godly way. You accept yourself and your situation. At this point, you walk in *victory* most of the time because you have changed your lifestyle and are going on with a new vision from the Lord as a single person.

Chapter 4

SIX STAGES OF DIVORCE

There are at least six well-recognized stages of divorce one experiences that overlap. They are not necessarily experienced in the same order or degree of intensity. Experts say these six stages and the process during the transitional period that happens when facing up to the divorce may take more than two years.[25]

Emotional Divorce

Initially, a person begins to notice an *Emotional divorce* from the "ex." This detachment from caring and loving often starts during the marriage. One partner may be more aware of it than the other; nevertheless, it is a red flag. I am a proponent of getting both professional and lay counseling throughout one's life whether married or not, as needed. This is definitely one of those times, before the situation becomes unsalvageable. If you are a Christian, then the counselors you are confiding in should be Christians too. Their value system should be similar to yours. However, if you are married to someone who is not a Christian, in order to be fair to both of you, perhaps you and the other partner may be able to reach a compromise, and go to a secular professional counselor. That way, the other partner will not feel like the scales are tipped in your favor. Agreeing to this initially may open the door for the Lord to soften their heart, and they may eventually agree to counseling with a pastor or other spiritual leader. This will give you both a more balanced perspective.

> **PERSONAL EXAMPLE:** At this point in my life, I went to my pastor first. He very wisely told me to ask my husband if *he* would be willing to choose a professional counselor we could *both* go to and if he would *also* be willing for me to go to my pastor for counseling. Although he would not agree to go to my pastor, he did agree to joint counseling with a counselor of his choice, and I continued with my pastor in counseling. It was a good compromise.

Sometimes a decision is made for a trial separation, and one partner leaves the home. When a separation occurs, whether a divorce is already contemplated or not, children will sense something is going on, o r interpret it improperly, and not actually understand it. For that reason, they need to be told the truth. The explanation should be simple and basic, but not hidden from them. If you try to sugarcoat the separation, the child will think they are the problem. They need to be reassured that both parents love *them* regardless, even though they cannot peacefully live together.

Once one parent moves out, there is a major disruption in the household that affects everyone. Roles of even children change, often unintentionally. This is where a child may take on an adult's burden that they are not created for. Rules and expectations change on everyone's part.

Do not be surprised if embarrassment is experienced by you when others find out. It is better if you face the situation head on with your family and friends. Be pro-active in sharing your situation with others, deliberately seeking not to be negative about the other person.

Legal Divorce

The second stage is the actual *Legal divorce*. Legal papers are prepared, and if one parent has not yet moved out, then this is usually the time when they do. The problem here is that often a false understanding about how you will feel arises. If you expect the legality issue to solve your feelings problem, you will be blindsided at every turn. The legal papers release you as far as the law is concerned, yet there is no provision in the law for feelings to be released. This is where good friends come in, friends who can support you emotionally without taking sides, friends who can see what is going on with your children and can address those situations.

Chapter 4

Economic Divorce

Next is the *Economic divorce*. The reality of the impending divorce usually happens when one person moves out, but if it has not, this is where the rubber meets the road, when it hits your pocketbook and lifestyle changes occur. This includes division of property, finances, and (yes) even pets. A loss of a pet may be even more devastating to a child than losing the parent, especially if abuse has been a part of the home.

Sometimes a stay-at-home mother must now seek employment. All of these decisions can bring new challenges of how to handle resentments, hostilities, and revenge. The more you can amicably agree upon, the less stress you and your children will experience. Your children need to feel as secure as possible, especially during this time of transition. Perhaps, rather than downsizing by selling the family home and dividing the proceeds, consider that it might be best for the parent who has physical custody of the children to remain in the home at least temporarily until the dust settles. The less things change around the children, the more stability they will experience.

Co-parental Divorce

The next stage is the *Co-parental divorce*. This pertains to where the parents are divorced from each other but are not divorced from their children. It is easy to have a loss of perspective and forget you are not divorcing the children. Unfortunately, this is often where the child does feel he is being divorced from one parent or the other. Keep your feelings and issues about the other parent to yourself. Do not project them onto your child. Do not attack or blame the other parent, justify your actions or force the child to take sides. Be the mature adult. They are just children.

> **HANDY HINT for both parents:** As you consider the *financial* aspects, and the emotions wrapped around those possessions, it is easy to forget a child's *feelings*. Keep in mind what is best for the children.

Community Divorce

Another stage is the *Community divorce* which is characterized by loneliness from society. Your status as a couple has changed, yet you are not totally single, because you are a single parent. You have lost your partner and possibly other significant people too. Other couples may see the divorced person as a threat to their marriage if they are insecure in themselves or insecure in their own marriages. Remember, the loneliness you feel is not usually a rejection of the divorced person (you) per se'. It is instead a result of your position in society in general. This is a painful time of watershed with friends and family: who will support you, who will take sides, etc.?

Psychological Divorce

The last state is *Psychological divorce* which means you are becoming autonomous from the influence of the "ex," their thoughts and actions. This is a time of intense emotional adjustment and grieving, yet it is also the time to learn how to become a whole and healthy person. By discovering who YOU really are, you will be able to take what you have learned into your parenting as well as any future relationships whether or not that includes marriage.

CHAPTER 5

Life after Divorce

PREPARATION FOR MARRIAGE OR REMARRIAGE

Often we believe the lies generated in our minds or those implanted by Satan, and then we become deceived. Ask the Lord to show you how the enemy will lie to you about eligible men. Either it is hard for a single mom to believe she will ever marry or remarry because there are so few eligible Christian men, or the single mother is being attracted to almost every man they come in contact with that looks as though he might be eligible. The Lord has a plan for you, and if it is His will for you to marry, the fact that you have a child or many children will not be a hindrance. You will not need to seek out eligible men since the Lord will be preparing one for you. Do not settle for less than what the Lord has intended by jumping at the first relationship that seems promising.

Marriage is such an important decision that the Lord will not leave you on your own to decide whether or not this one is the "right one" for you. As a single mother, now the question becomes a question of deciding if this is the right one for you *and* your child. God wants the best for both of you. Only He truly knows what (and who) that is. If you seek Him, He will give you the confirmation through His Word, in your heart, and through an agreement of counsel.

A common question I have heard many times, especially if you have been a single mother for quite awhile is: "I want to get married. Why doesn't the Lord send me a mate?" The Word says He will provide all our *needs*, according to His riches in Christ Jesus.

> *But my God shall supply all your need according to his riches in glory by Christ Jesus (Philippians 4:19 KJV).*

If you are not trying to work something out in your own fleshly efforts, when it becomes a *need* for a single mother to be married and a *need* for your children to have a stepfather, God will provide. Until then, I believe it is a want, and Christ can fulfill all your wants by Him being your husband. He does not want you trying to work it out by your own efforts. He has what is best for you in mind, not just a *good* answer, but the *best* answer.

Remember God is preparing your future spouse for you, and if he has children, God is preparing his children for your family. God is not working just on behalf of your heart's desire; He always prepares both hearts of the parties involved. While waiting for its fulfillment, do not despair if marriage is your heart's desire. Just remember, God is working behind the scenes.

In the interim, He may have a plan to give you the spiritual gift of singleness. Spiritual gifts are given to those who have accepted Jesus as their Lord and Savior. The spiritual gift of singleness is defined as being single or unmarried *and* living a celibate lifestyle for the Lord. While you are waiting, you may want to consider asking Him for this spiritual gift.

Jesus talked about three situations where someone might remain single.

> *'Not everyone can accept this statement,' Jesus said 'Only those whom God helps. Some are born as eunuchs, some have been made that way by others, and some choose not to marry for the sake of the Kingdom of Heaven. Let anyone accept this who can' (Matthew 19:11-12 NLT).*

These three categories are: (1) Being born a eunuch,[26] (2) being castrated or (3) choosing not to marry for a season in order to serve God.

I believe the third choice is a supernatural gift God will give to you if you ask Him, and if your circumstances warrant it, such as, being a single parent wanting to abstain from sex and serve God. This is not something you decide to do on your own strength.

If you are wondering whether or not this might be something that would enhance your life while you are single, or help you while you are waiting for a mate, here are some questions that may show you the advantage of having this spiritual gift.

- ✓ Have you experienced those natural God-given sexual desires as a single mother and feel they are a distraction to your desire to please and serve God?
- ✓ Are you struggling to keep your thoughts, motives, and acts pure toward the opposite sex?
- ✓ Is there a fear in the back of your mind that you will fall into a sexual temptation, so strong that it may hinder your ability to develop a normal, yet platonic relationship with men in general?
- ✓ Are you attracted to the opposite sex to the point of distraction or obsession and want to experience freedom in this area?

If any of these situations apply, if you are a Christian, you might consider asking God for the spiritual gift of being single.

The secular world or carnal Christians who try to deny themselves in the sexual area become frustrated and fall into temptation. For them, it is hard to remain celibate until they find the person they want to marry, since they do not have anything or anyone else to replace those desires. This does not have to be the case for a Christian. God never asks us to do something and then not enable us to be able to do it. That would be cruel. Instead, He offers us this as a gift that we can draw upon.

God knows we have sexual desires because He created us with sexual feelings. However, He wants us to control them or get married. Paul, who was single at the time he wrote to the Corinthians, speaks to this issue.

> *Now regarding the questions you asked in your letter. Yes, it is good to abstain from sexual relations (I Corinthians 7:1 NLT).*

He continues:

> *I say this as a concession, not as a command. But I wish everyone were single, just as I am. Yet each person has a special gift from God, of one kind or another. So I say to those who aren't married and to widows—it's better to stay unmarried, just as I am. But if they can't control themselves,*

they should go ahead and marry. It's better to marry than to burn with lust (I Corinthians 7:6-9 NLT).

> **PERSONAL EXAMPLE:** During my 30's, I was on staff with a ministry and surrounded by eligible Christian men. The ratio was three men to one woman, and this gift of singleness enabled me to be focused totally on the Lord. I set my face like a flint towards being sold out to the Lord, and I learned to relate to these men of God as my friends instead of eligible mates.

After my first marriage, I had two children to raise, and I wanted to focus on them and on serving the Lord without distractions.

As I observed other single parents struggle with the dating game and opposite-sex relationships, I realized those things were not beneficial for me or my children. I never formally asked God for the gift of singleness; however, somewhere along the line, I realized that it had been given to me. I did not ask for it, but He knew my heart. I just wanted to serve Jesus. This gift lasted five years until I remarried. When I remarried, I did not need that gift any longer, and the Lord supernaturally took it away.

If you receive this gift, you will discover peace, joy, and contentment with being single. You will not be hindered by a sexual tension that many singles combat. You will not be looking at every eligible guy and wondering, "Is this the one for me?"

With this spiritual gift, your passion for Jesus will outweigh any passion for the opposite sex during this season in your life. This frees you to be yourself around the opposite sex, instead of scoping them out. It will release you to join in activities based on your interests, as opposed to joining or not joining a group or activity because of potential male attachments.

Make the decision before becoming involved in a relationship where you will draw the line physically. Then stand firm in that decision in your heart. Discuss this with the person you are dating. If the potential mate is unwilling to abide by your line, then do not continue that relationship. If they do not honor your desires on this point, they will not honor your desires on other levels after marriage.

As a single mother, now your decisions are autonomous. You have more power and influence in a relationship prior to marriage than afterwards. If you experience a "deal-breaker" during the dating time, you can more easily walk away from a relationship, and the other person knows that.

> **REMEMBER:** Two things change a relationship — money and sex.

One advantage of being single is that you can serve God without consulting a partner. Your choices will still affect your children. However, it is easier to serve God when you are single than married. The more people there are in your life, the more complicated life becomes. Relationships are just that way. You can focus better when there are fewer distractions in a job or ministry. If you remain single, your vision is not as easily hindered as when you are married. So why not ask God to give you the spiritual gift of being single that He offers? Paul says it this way:

> *In the same way, a woman who is no longer married or has never been married can be devoted to the Lord and holy in body and in spirit. But a married woman has to think about her earthly responsibilities and how to please her husband. I am saying this for your benefit, not to place restrictions on you. I want you to do whatever will help you serve the Lord best, with as few distractions as possible* (I Corinthians 7:34-35 NLT).

I have been single without children, married with children, and a single mother, and I agree with Paul. Life is simpler, and it is easier serving the Lord as a single person without children. Being married, as wonderful as it is, complicates matters because you have someone else to consider. Adding children into the mix brings even more responsibilities.

A single parent is no longer a single person, nor are they a part of a married couple. They do not fit in either category. They are in-between these two groups because they have a child. Since the priority should be that of meeting the practical, emotional, and spiritual aspects of your children, a single parent should be living a life that exemplifies virtuous habits in both your lifestyle and your thoughts. Your child needs you at this time in their life more than ever. A relationship with someone new takes time and energy away from them.

Although 48% of all first marriages will eventually end in divorce,[27] the statistics are much higher for subsequent marriages: 70%+ of remarriages involving children end in dissolution within 5 ½ years.[28]

Sadly, divorce is equally prevalent both inside and outside the church. Considering our culture today, although it may seem harder at the time, remaining single while minor children are still in the home may be a better option than remarriage.

You may not want to remarry; therefore, if the Lord has *not* brought someone into your life, do not let yourself feel condemned during this season. If you have committed your life to Him, it is up to Him to change your circumstances. It is not your "job" to find a partner.

Take advantage of this time to devote your efforts to becoming spiritually strong by learning to control your sexual desires and seeking the Lord for your unique ministry during this "season" of celibacy. Then you can be assured that this season in your life is God's will for you.

On the other hand, the Lord has given us the institution of marriage. He created Eve in the Garden of Eden to be Adam's helpmate. Therefore, it was His design for two to walk as one in a marriage relationship creating a family. He is the God of second chances (and third and fourth, etc.), so if He brings someone into your life, I believe, under those circumstances, a Christian single mother could be married. The main criteria are that she should only marry another believer as shown in the two verses below.

> *A woman is bound to her husband as long as he lives. But if her husband dies, she is free to marry anyone she wishes, but he must belong to the Lord (I Corinthians 7:39 NIV).*
>
> *Do not be mismated with unbelievers. For what partnership have righteousness and iniquity? Or what fellowship has light with darkness? (II Corinthians 6:14 RSV).*

Therefore, if you do desire to marry or remarry while your child is still a minor, you can pray in confidence for a mate and not feel condemned while waiting. This is also Paul's advice to young widows whether they are mothers or not.

> *So I advise these younger widows to marry again, have children, and take care of their own homes. Then the enemy will not be able to say anything against them (I Timothy 5:14 NLT).*

Meanwhile, you and your child have options that you will not have when you get married, so enjoy those while you can. God wants you to experience an abundant life where you are now as a single mother. He does not want you to always be looking around the corner for the next person that you imagine might deliver you out of your circumstances. He wants you to have a fulfilling and satisfying life now. You do not have to wait. The abundant life Jesus has planned for you is available now for the asking. Jesus said:

> *The thief's purpose is to steal and kill and destroy. My purpose is to give them a rich and satisfying life (John 10:10 NLT).*

As you develop and grow into the woman Christ wants you to become, you will become the woman a Christian man is looking for and wants.

> *A woman's heart should be so hidden in Christ that a man should have to seek Him first to find her.*[29]

In I Timothy 5:2-16, Paul speaks of different characteristics a Godly woman should be exhibiting in her life: Taking care of her children and grandchildren; taking care of her parents; placing her hope in God, spending a lot of time in prayer. A result of doing of these things is that she is well-respected by everyone. Furthermore, he asks:

"Has she brought up her children in a good way, been kind to strangers, served other Christians humbly, helped those who are in trouble, and been available to do good things?" These are excellent qualities to gain in preparation for getting married. As you are developing these qualities in your life, your perspective will begin to change. You will reprioritize the things you want in a mate. Some things will become more important to you; other things will drop out of the picture.

You will want someone compatible to your lifestyle. In various partnerships, God says it is important not to "team up" or become "unequally yoked" with those who are not believers.

> Don't team up with those who are unbelievers. How can righteousness be a partner with wickedness? How can light live with darkness? (II Corinthians 6:14 NLT).

One way to "team up" is for a believer to marry a non-believer, something God warns against. But, it is also possible to become "unequally yoked" to a believer. Even if you have the same faith, you can be mismatched. If you are a woman who has had leadership responsibilities, then the best scenario for you is that the believer you marry should be experienced in similar areas of accountability and authority.

In reality, you are presently the head of your household, and your future mate needs to have had experience in similar ways, in order to successfully become the head of your household. This is a huge responsibility because you come with a ready-made functioning family. This new aspect of responsibility is not something he will have time to grow into even it you have dated for a long time. It will be instantaneous. One day you are both single and after marriage, the very first day, he receives a new physical and spiritual role as well as new spiritual authority as head of household.

God wants the best for you, and while He is preparing you for a future spouse, He is also preparing your future spouse for you. God picked out spouses in the Bible, and He can and does do the same today. He chose Eve for Adam, Rebekah for Isaac, and Joseph for Mary.

Mary conceived by the Holy Spirit as a virgin while engaged to Joseph. If this had become public information, under the law, Joseph would have had every right to divorce her, or she could have been stoned because it appeared she had been adulterous.[30] However, Joseph was told by an angel that she was chosen to conceive supernaturally and to marry her anyway. We see the story in Matthew 1.

> *Now the birth of Jesus Christ was as follows: After His mother Mary was betrothed to Joseph, before they came together, she was found with child of the Holy Spirit. Then Joseph her husband, being a just man, and not wanting to make her a public example, was minded to put her away secretly. But while he thought about these things, behold, an angel of the Lord appeared to him in a dream, saying, 'Joseph, son of David, do not be afraid to take to you Mary your wife, for that which is conceived in her is of the Holy Spirit. And she will bring forth a Son, and you shall call His name JESUS, for He will save His people from their sins.' So all this was done that it might be fulfilled which was spoken by the Lord through the prophet, saying: 'Behold, the virgin shall be with child, and bear a Son, and they shall call His name Immanuel,' which is translated, 'God with us.' Then Joseph, being aroused from sleep, did as the angel of the Lord commanded him and took to him his wife, and did not know her till she had brought forth her firstborn Son. And he called His name JESUS (Matthew 1:18-25 NKJV).*

Mary probably dealt with shame and embarrassment as her condition became public; nevertheless, she and Joseph faced it head on. She had a pure heart and was willing to be used of the Lord.

> *Then Mary said, 'Behold the maidservant of the Lord! Let it be to me according to your word' (Luke 1:38(a) NKJV).*

The last time Joseph is mentioned in the Bible, Jesus was 12 years old. For that reason, there is speculation on my part that perhaps Mary was a single mom later in her life, and perhaps a

Chapter 5

single mom of several children. In Matthew, the scribes tell us that after she gave birth to Jesus, she had other children.

> *'Is this not the carpenter's son? Is not His mother called Mary? And His brothers James, Joses, Simon, and Judas? And His sisters, are they not all with us?' (Matthew 13:55-56(a) NKJV).*

Knowing this, even before the foundation of the world, God had chosen her and honored her in a unique way.

God always wants to bless and honor you in a unique way. You do not know specifically how He intends to do that, but since He has a vested personal interest in you and your child, He desires to give you the very best. His heart beats with your heart. His heart breaks when you are hurting, and His heart rejoices when you are happy.

Since you have had a poor start at marriage or regarding a relationship, you might feel like a second-rate citizen or feel like you are damaged goods. God does not look at you that way. Guess what? Graham Cooke says it this way: "God is not disillusioned with you, because He never had any illusions of you in the first place! He knows exactly who you really are."[31]

Remember, He looks at you as His princess. You are beautiful to Him, and He wants the best for you. You are the "apple of His eye."

> *For thus says the LORD of hosts: '... for he who touches you touches the apple of His eye' (Zechariah 2:8 NKJV).*

Have you ever watched mothers at a playground? There are many children on the slides, on the teeter-totters, and in the sand pit. Yet, they keep their eyes, their attention on their child. They are not distracted by the other children playing. That is how God watches you. He is intensely interested in what you are doing at all times. He never takes his eyes off you.

If you understand how attentive He is towards you, how He wants the very best for you, you will not allow yourself to settle for second-best.

DATING

The secular world looks at dating differently than Christians. Listen to the words of Jesus.

> *But I say, anyone who even looks at a woman with lust in his eye has already committed adultery with her in his heart (Matthew 5:28 NLT).*

As hard as it may seem, if you are not divorced, you are not legally or spiritually free to date. Otherwise, you are committing adultery. When you date before the final divorce decree is granted, you are setting up that third party you are dating to covet another person (you). Not dating at this time is God's protection for you. He does not want to see your heart broken again.

Dating during this interim between separation and divorce only confuses the issues the Lord would like to develop in you and your family. You might not even know what concern or problem the Lord might put his finger on that He wants to change.

Years ago in California, the law was such that from the time of first filing the divorce papers, until you could be legally declared divorced, was a year. Now it is six months. This time is a drop in the bucket compared to the time it will take to be healed and restored from a broken relationship. It takes the heart, mind, and soul a lot longer than six months to bounce back and begin functioning normally again. To rush this process is spiritually, emotionally, and perhaps even physically detrimental. That is why there are so many rebound marriages.

People have a vacuum within them that they try to fill with anything and everything: food, drugs, alcohol, love, even material things. Trying to fill it with anything other than Jesus is impossible. Only Jesus can fill that hole—that vacuum in a person's soul.

This is a time for learning who you really were designed to be. The time after a separation and/or divorce is a perfect time to get your life more committed to the Lord, to get your priorities straight and to give your children the time they need. This takes effort and dedication. Remember the past can be forgiven, and it can become a learning process for the future. God forgives even divorce no matter whose *fault* it was. Divorce is not an unforgiveable sin.

You will not want this time to be a time of treading water. You want it to be productive. We learn the deepest heart lessons during the hardest times.

One's value system comes to the forefront much faster when children are a part of the package. The Word is clear about not marrying an unbeliever. Why tempt yourself and create a hard situation for yourself and your children by becoming involved with someone who does not share your faith?

> **REMEMBER:** Every date is a potential mate.

Do not settle for second best by dating a non-Christian. Even the most wonderful unbeliever has a different value system because the non-Christian cannot understand spiritual matters.

> *But people who aren't spiritual can't receive these truths from God's Spirit. It all sounds foolish to them and they can't understand it, for only those who are spiritual can understand what the Spirit means (I Corinthians 2:14 NLT).*

It is good to pray for a mate, except be sure to do it *privately*. It is not a good idea to involve the children in praying for a potential stepparent. This gives them a false hope and makes them become intently aware of expectations beyond their ability to comprehend because children do not have the capacity to understand time as adults do. Wait and let the Lord tell them personally when they should be praying for a stepparent. Then when the Lord lays it on their hearts, you can be sure He is doing the work, not you.

Do not forget to pray for your potential spouse's needs too, whether the person is known to you or not. We all get so wrapped up in our own lives, that we forget we are not the only ones in the equation. While you are waiting, it is good to remember that He is also shaping your potential spouse to be more like Jesus. The Lord works on both sides, with both parties.

Whether you are getting married for the first time or are contemplating remarriage, a great book to help you and your potential mate to avoid many pitfalls and to help you sort out whether or not this is the person for you and your child is called <u>Too Close Too Soon</u>, by Dr. Jim A. Talley and Dr. Bobbie Reed.

ENGAGEMENT

None of us think a relationship we are entering into will fail or else we would not even try. However, the fact is, relationships fail to come together as planned, and engagements are broken. I have seen many engagements broken, which can be good if it is not the right person. This is another area where you must be wise and proactive. Children do not need to deal with adult issues and will not have to, if we have protected them.

I have seen too many children with their hearts broken and confused by their parent's new budding relationship. When a new person comes along who seems to be spending a lot of time with their parent, the child is naturally going to start thinking this is going to be a permanent relationship. They can become disillusioned if a marriage does not come to pass. It causes insecurity in the child if they prematurely project any male or female to be their "daddy or mommy" when that person is not. If marriage does not occur, the child may be afraid to reach out to another male or female in their life in a healthy manner. This is especially true because the first parent has left, and now another person in their life is abandoning them and their parent.

When a new relationship in your life begins to develop, if your child seems to hold back or definitely opposes the new person in your life, consider this a "red flag." Up until now you have focused solely on your child. Now, because you are dividing your time and attention between them and the new person in your life, your child may resent this intrusion. This is normal.

Chapter 5

Therefore, it is also a time for you to go slowly. As time goes on, if the new person still does not seem to be winning your child over, there could be a good reason why.

As this relationship develops, and you become more emotionally involved, your common sense will be clouded by what you might consider love. You will view this new relationship more from an emotional standpoint, but your child will be assessing the situation in a different way, so pay attention to their reaction to this new person. This does not mean your child will have the final say in the decision to marry; although, it does mean you should make yourself aware of why they are acting out.

The winning over should be a natural result of spending time with the family as a whole, not spending time with the child alone. Once again, this new change gets their hopes up, and the single parent does not need to put their children through all this drama until something is concrete.

Once formally engaged, the relationship should be described to the children that this is a "special friend," and then unfold the future plans slowly so they can be part of the process. Physical affection around the children should be kept discreet.

During this stage, your child may truly be won over by your "special friend," or they may start acting out in a negative manner. If they do not seem to like the person, it could be jealousy, or there could be a valid reason why they do not like them. Again, take this as a "red flag", and talk to your child. If they are acting out, you need to become more aware of what is really happening with them, what they are feeling, and why. There may be a good reason that you cannot see because you are "in love."

Do not allow any man or woman to play daddy or mommy, even in role innuendos, such as referring to "the children" as if they were "our" children, even if you are engaged. Again, this sets the child up for disappointment if the projected marriage fails to materialize.

I have seen many situations during the engagement period where the child is already calling the potential stepparent "daddy or mommy." The person you have a relationship with is not the stepparent until you say "I do" at the altar. I would discourage use of these endearing terms until after marriage. These terms give a title of respect that is very powerful after marriage if it has not been watered down beforehand by casual use.

After you are married, you can let your child decide whether or not he wants to call them "daddy." If your "ex" is still in the picture, your child may feel using this term is disrespectful or dishonoring to their natural parent. They may decide to use the stepparent's first name instead, or a name distinguishing that stepparent from their "daddy" by calling him "dad" or "father" or "papa" instead.

In the event your "ex" remarries, this dynamic still applies. Let your child decide on their own what to call the new stepparent. Do not force them either way.

Whether it is you who remarries or your "ex," the stepparent never replaces either of the child's parents. To introduce the stepparent as the new "daddy" or "mommy" is not fair to the child. It can cause confusion, and may make them feel they are betraying their natural parent by using that title. It is better to tell your child that their new stepparent is not *replacing* their natural parent. They *add* to the family. This will do a lot towards alleviating any fears on the child's part of feeling like they will betray their natural parent if they start to enjoy the new dynamics the stepparent brings into the family whether it is your family or your "ex's" family.

If and when your "ex" remarries, if possible, talk these issues through with the "ex" and the new stepparent ahead of time. It would be wise to cultivate a good relationship with the new stepparent. This will help alleviate fears or concerns you may have that might creep up about their living situation, and will give you more credibility in the sight of the new stepparent. Being civil to the other parent's new spouse will go far with your "ex" and smooth over the transitional visitation times.

Chapter 5

Expect that your child will act differently when they come back from a visit with the other parent. This will go a long way in helping you be patient. Their rules may be different, and the child is going to push the boundaries with you each time. You will need to re-establish your expectations with your child.

If possible, try to discuss rules and boundaries with your "ex" and attempt to make them consistent between yourselves. Hopefully, discussing this will alleviate a lot of confusion on the part of your child and make re-entry more peaceful when they return from a visit with the other parent.

I do not believe, (and this is just an opinion) that you should allow any man or woman to discipline your child corporally if you are not married. When a man enters your life, as a stressed-out single mother, it may be easier to hand over the corporal discipline to him. But, easier is not always wiser. I think this is something you need to be very careful about. Be faithful to keep this matter in prayer.

Single Mom??? What Now???

CHAPTER 6

Life as a Single Mom

UNUSUAL SITUATIONS AND SOLUTIONS

You probably have asked yourself, "Where and how do I fit in socially? Who am I besides the mother?"

This dilemma comes up early in the life of a single mom. You ask yourself, "Is my role to be that of a mother, or a father, or both?" I found out real quickly that I was expected to operate in both roles; yet as a woman, and as a practical matter, there were naturally certain limitations. As far as time and energy were concerned, I was the only one around, and therefore, my *children* expected me to fulfill both those roles. Although they never expressed that expectation; that is just the way it is when you become a single parent. You are the one they depend upon.

Although it is not usually outwardly expressed by others, or even inwardly acknowledged by the single parent, most single parents are inaccurately expected to be a mother + father + ??? (you fill in the blank). A single mother is expected by *society* to fulfill the role of both parents, just by default. Most of our culture does not usually think this through. Nevertheless, practically speaking, a single mother cannot be the "be all and end all" to her family no matter how hard she tries. However, God in His infinite mercy has an answer.

I quickly realized I had a double responsibility, but I did not know that I could receive a double amount of grace as well. The Bible calls it a "double portion."

> *And so it was, when they had crossed over, that Elijah said to Elisha, 'Ask! What may I do for you, before I am taken away from you?' Elisha said, 'Please let a double portion of your spirit be upon me' (II Kings 2:9 NKJV).*

When I read this, I knew in my heart this is what I needed. I needed a "double portion" of His spirit and His love. The Lord never gives us too much to handle. He expects us to go to Him to get the answers on how to raise our children. He wants to bless us and give us more of Himself. No matter how much we have been given by the Lord, He wants to give us more. Frequently, we view God as being stingy, yet His nature is to be very generous.

Since I had a double portion of responsibility, I asked for that double portion of His Spirit to be able to raise my children, and God granted it to me for that season in my life. If you ask in faith, He will give you that double portion as well.

A FISH OUT OF WATER?

This is a stage where you feel *in limbo*, and you are. So don't fight it; eventually this feeling will pass. Previously, when we looked at one of God's promises for a single mom, we saw that He will establish her boundary; however, the first part of this same verse talks about being proud.

> *The LORD will destroy the house of the proud, But He will establish the boundary of the widow (Proverbs 15:25 NKJV).*

He will establish a new life for you if you humble yourself. This new life may look entirely different than you imagine it to be right now. Prepare yourself for an adventure.

Often in this stage, we think we need *permission* to make changes, no matter how small. Giving yourself permission could be as simple as removing a picture (one that you never liked anyway) from a room, or starting to buy food that you did not before because you deferred to your "ex's" food choices, or it could be as big as redecorating your house in *your* style. Once you begin to take charge of even the smallest matters, then healing will begin to take place in larger matters, and your other relationships will become more balanced.

The reason you feel like "a fish out of water," like you do not belong, is for the reason that whether you are a single mother by choice or by some sort of abandonment, you are not married, and you are not readily accepted into the single lifestyle because you have children.

You need not wait until someone invites you to go to a function or join an activity. If you do not take the initiative, you may wait your life away. The Lord does not expect you to put your life on hold until you get married or your child grows up. You are not being punished for being a single mom. In God's eyes, you are a complete person *now*, and you still have a family. Do not let the enemy rob you of this understanding and make you think you are not complete either as a single person or as a family just because you are single. God established families through marriage, and the birth of your child added to that family. You may not be a traditional nuclear family; nevertheless, you are still a family.

Be kind to yourself, and your child will benefit. Learn to love the Lord Jesus, and then let the Lord love you. I encourage you to take time for yourself. This cannot be stressed enough.

> **PERSONAL EXAMPLE:** One way I let the Lord love me is by lifting my hands, often when I am singing. I raise my hands to my "daddy," and I picture Him lifting me up. I say to myself, "Lift me up daddy and put me on your lap." That action puts His love for me in perspective.

Most Christian single parents carry the "false guilt" of believing they have to make up for all their child has lost or are losing as a result of a divorce or separation. Often this is exhibited by buying them something every time they go to the store. It is subtle, but the unspoken, yet driving motivation, is that some *thing* will make up for the some *one* that is missing. Well, it does not. The single parent needs to resolve their false guilt by realizing they cannot cover all of the bases they are expected to, and that is OK, because God can and will fill in those gaps in ways you cannot imagine.

The other parent who is not there physically on a regular basis also needs to recognize that their true motivation for buying things or spoiling the child in lieu of spending time with the child is being driven by their guilt feelings.

Often this "guilt phase" sets in after they have dealt with their own perceived guilt of failing as a *partner*, and a single parent begins to redouble their efforts to *not* fail as the *parent*. This is a devious mental trap Satan uses, and it is not usually recognized by those outside the immediate family. The single mother tries to make up for the absent parent by redoubling her efforts to cater to the children. The children become more demanding and the single mother caves in. If this cycle continues, the children become spoiled and expect others to cater to them. Continuing to try harder to *not* fail as the *parent* will create all kinds of grief for the single parent, and mental or physical repercussions will occur.

Once again, God has the answer. The prescription for the single mother (*especially* a single mother) is to set aside time for herself by figuring out ways to lift her own spirit on a regular basis *apart* from her children. By doing this, peace will replace guilt, and you will become a better mother.

Remember, it is all a process and does not happen overnight. You will immediately begin to feel better if you start to take care of yourself. Ultimately, God is the only one who can totally remove your guilt and set you free to be who He designed you to be. Sin (disobedience to God) causes guilt, yet God has an answer.

> *He has removed our sins as far from us as the east is from the west (Psalm 103:12 NLT).*

You just have to ask God to forgive you, and He will. Then you need to remember to forgive yourself.

A SINGLE GRANDMOTHER

Another scenario that is becoming more and more prevalent in our society is the *grand*mother who is raising their *grand*child alone. Once your children leave the home and have their own children, one does not usually envision they will be raising their grandchildren full time, particularly alone. Perhaps death has taken one or both parents, the grandchild's parents have been unable or unwilling to fulfill their responsibilities, or perhaps have even abandoned their children, and the *grand*mother is the one raising them. If this is your situation, just remember God knew before the foundation of the world that this would be *your* journey as well as your *grandchild's* journey. He knows what is best for you and your grandchild. You can probably relate to most of the single mother's situations, and the promises God gives to a single mother can be appropriated by you as a grandmother. There is no testimony without a test, and He will never give you more than you can handle. He wants to walk with you every step of the way.

When you raised your children, you probably realized there were a lot of things you wished you could change. Now you can. Where would they be without you? Maybe they would be in the government's system? You are a *gift* to them from God! Never forget that. They may not realize that now, but they will when they grow up. This is God giving you a second opportunity to lavish the grandchild you are raising with love and not make the same mistakes you did with your children.

God does not keep score, and He is giving you the privilege of leading your grandchild to the Lord. Do not read the following passage too fast. God is speaking about your "children's children," not your children. In the day-to-day activities, we often lose track of the fact that even our grandchildren are given to us to influence so another soul can be introduced to the Lord.

> *But the love of the LORD remains forever with those who fear him. His salvation extends to the children's children, of those who are faithful to his covenant, of those who obey his commandments (Psalm 103:17-18 NLT).*

FINDING A CHURCH HOME

As a divorcee' in the 1950's, my mother was a minority in society in general and in church more specifically. As a result, she sent us to church although she did not attend herself. By the 1960's, some churches began to view divorce in a different light. They began to realize that divorce was not the ultimate sin, and they began to accept a divorced person into the church family without making them feel guilty.

Today there is no excuse for a single parent not to be in a community of believers that accepts them and their children. In this day and age, there are plenty of churches who do not create barriers for divorced or single parents.

The criteria for choosing a church home should be that it is a Bible-believing and a Bible-practicing church.

There may be limitations for a divorced woman in some leadership positions within some churches, although in general, most churches accept divorced people. If you feel judged where you go to church, especially as a divorcee', find a place where you can belong, a place where you can feel like family. You need all the support you can get at this time and so does your child. Find a pastor who can relate to you. You need an extended family, and a loving church will provide that for you. There are plenty of churches that preach the Word and who understand and accept single parents.

SPIRITUAL COUNSEL

Ideally, counsel is not to tell you what to do. On the contrary, it is to confirm what the Lord has already shown you. Therefore, it is incumbent upon you to be seeking the Lord on your own for answers to your situation and upcoming decisions. I have seen many single mothers become prey for cults. As a rule, they have very little spiritual input and may not know the Bible very well themselves. Consequently, to protect yourself and your children, you need to develop a lifestyle of prayer, Godly counsel, and reading God's Word. If you know and do what it says, life will be less confusing, and you will avoid many pitfalls.

No one person should have the power to control another's life, even verbally; nevertheless, Godly input is invaluable. The Bible has numerous references to counsel being established through more than one person. Here is just one:

> ...*In the mouth of two or three witnesses shall every word be established (II Corinthians 13:1(b) KJV).*

It is safer to share with others who are mature in the Word, who can walk alongside you, than to isolate yourself.

SPIRITUAL AUTHORITY

Everyone lives under some kind of authority structure: the government, traffic laws, a job, a school, etc. Yielding or submitting to the rules and regulations that are in place for those particular agencies keeps everything running smoothly and lessens conflict.

However, in our culture, the word "submit" often brings negative connotations, especially because it cuts across our fleshly grain. We want to do *it* our way—whatever *it* is.

One Biblical definition of "submit" means "to yield to one's admonition or advice," or "to adapt." This is God's idea of submitting, and it feels differently because it is. As Christians, we are called the bride of Christ, and for the reason that Christ is our husband, we submit to His advice, or adapt to the counsel He gives us, whether in the Bible or by the Holy Spirit.

When you are married, you are to submit to your own husband. However, since a single mother or widow does not have an earthly husband to care for her or to advise her, she can submit or adapt directly to Jesus.

> *Wives, submit to your own husbands, as to the Lord (Ephesians 5:22 NKJV).*

He is going to treat you better than you can imagine. He will never ask you to sin. You can willingly, even joyfully submit to God and be confident He will protect you.

However, without a physical husband, who is a single mom's physical spiritual authority after Jesus? After all, you may have questions and situations come up where you need counsel. You are then to look to your church's pastor, elders or any other spiritual authority which your church has established as directed in the Hebrews passage below. When your spiritual leaders are in proper submission to God, exciting and wonderful things happen.

> *Obey your spiritual leaders and do what they say. Their work is to watch over your souls, and they know they are accountable to God. Give them reason to do this joyfully and*

not with sorrow. That would certainly not be for your benefit (Hebrews 13:17 NLT).

In II Kings 4, we read how the following widowed single mother with two sons was miraculously provided for financially through unusual means. Before her husband died, her husband had been in proper authority under his spiritual leader, the prophet Elisha. That is why she felt confident to go to Elisha and plead her cause to him; and he responded in a Godly manner because he knew he was accountable to God.

> *One day the widow of a member of the group of prophets came to Elisha and cried out, 'My husband who served you is dead, and you know how he feared the LORD. But now a creditor has come, threatening to take my two sons as slaves.' 'What can I do to help you?' Elisha asked. 'Tell me, what do you have in the house?' 'Nothing at all, except a flask of olive oil,' she replied. And Elisha said, 'Borrow as many empty jars as you can from your friends and neighbors. Then go into your house with your sons and shut the door behind you. Pour olive oil from your flask into the jars, setting each one aside when it is filled.' So she did as she was told. Her sons kept bringing jars to her, and she filled one after another. Soon every container was full to the brim! 'Bring me another jar,' she said to one of her sons. 'There are not any more!' he told her. And then the olive oil stopped flowing. When she told the man of God what had happened, he said to her, 'Now sell the olive oil and pay your debts, and you and your sons can live on what is left over' (II Kings 4:1-7 NLT).*

Since Elisha was obedient to God, this single mother felt safe to ask for his help. When she was counseled by him, she had confidence in his instructions, and she obeyed. As a result, she was able to garner enough money by selling the oil, which the Lord had miraculously multiplied, to pay her bills. This example shows a healthy relationship between Elisha and the widow.

All women need to be aware of not projecting any male's counseling relationship into being something more than Godly caring and counsel. However, a single mother is more vulnerable and must be especially watchful in these situations. Even in a professional or pastoral capacity, when a man shows a concern for her and her child's well-being, she can mistakenly entertain false thoughts about that person's feelings toward her in that relationship.

All counseling situations should be kept within the framework of God's agapē love and boundaries. This same principle can be applied to all men counseling women, whether the men are in a formal position of authority or not.

Single moms need a man's point of view, but if the man in this situation is not directing you to another woman for counsel and friendship, this can become an unhealthy relationship. This is a common snare that can be avoided with the establishment of boundaries on both sides *prior* to establishing any relationship and adhering to those mutually agreed-upon boundaries.

The best way to avoid this trap and avoid an unhealthy relationship is to involve other mature, Godly women in listening to your heart as well. Is there someone you already know who fits this role?

FINANCIAL CONDITIONS

Jesus said the poor are always with you.

> 'For you have the poor with you always, but Me you do not have always' (Matthew 26:11 NKJV).

I think this verse certainly includes single mothers. She is often on some kind of government aid, does not get regular child support, if any, and few have well-paying jobs. Even if they do have a well-paying job, they have the added expense of a babysitter as a *basic* need, which is entirely different than working and paying a babysitter or nanny on two salaries. Often this financial change is sudden and not planned for. Their standard of living is usually less than a married couple. They usually need the same living space as if married, yet without the advantage of two salaries. They need sitters for both work and a social life as they do not have a spouse to step in.

Chapter 6

Your responsibility as a single mother is to be wise with the money you do receive, and ask and expect God to fill in the difference.

When your child asks for something, rather than telling them you do not have the money, you could say, "We choose to spend our money differently," or "We have what we need: food, a roof over our heads, and clothing." Another answer could be, "We can ask Jesus to give us ..." (you fill in the blank of what your child is asking for.) An advantage to answering this way gives both you and your children the opportunity to see God answer prayer.

> **PERSONAL EXAMPLE:** Whenever I was low on groceries, particularly meat, I would remind the Lord of what He said about Himself in Psalm 50:10: "...I own the cattle on a thousand hills...," and I would ask the Lord to sell a side of beef for me. That would increase my faith, and then I would wait to see how God would provide. It was not always beef, but He never failed to feed me and my children.

> **HANDY HINT to others:** Another excellent way to minister to a single mother's needs is to offer to trade babysitting, or better yet, sit for free.

REPAIRING THINGS THAT BREAK

Most single moms are usually not able to assemble toys from scratch, or fix major things that break, nor do they have the money to pay to have it done. This can be a real frustration without a man around.

So, here is what I did. I kept an ongoing repair list just like I would for a husband's "honey-do" list. Then I prayed. From time to time, someone would offer to help in some way, and I was prepared with my handy-dandy list. The Lord would always send someone in His timing with the exact expertise I needed for whatever task needed to be done.

> **HANDY HINT for a handy person:** Since so many toys come unassembled at Christmas and birthdays, you might want to be proactive and offer your skills before those occasions arrive. This will alleviate any single mother's worries about how she is going to get the toys assembled, and it will touch her heart that someone thought of her need before she expressed it.

HOLIDAYS

Holidays usually bring family feelings to the surface when you are a single mother long before the nuclear family is thinking of holidays. This is an especially hard time if the child visits the other parent. Often doubt, depression, and rejection sets in early in the holiday season. Correctly, or incorrectly, you may think you will be alone on that special day.

This was the time I found I had to be very proactive. I began making plans earlier than other families usually did. I either invited other single mothers over for the holidays or made plans to be with another family. I created new traditions differently from how we celebrated each holiday when I was married. Children need to be able to look forward to the holidays in a positive way just as much as a single mother does.

A word of caution: Do not fall into the trap of competing with the other parent and trying to make your holiday more expensive or spectacular. Remember: Time spent with your child and others is more important than things.

Chapter 6

> **HANDY HINT for families who know a single mother:** If you want to bless a single mother, think of them before the holiday season, and extend an invitation to join your family EARLY in the holiday season. It is never too early, even if they give you an unclear response. It will make them feel better about themselves and the holidays to know that someone was thinking of them and not just as an after-thought.

COMMON QUESTIONS DURING ADJUSTMENT PERIOD

During a separation or divorce there are many practical questions that come up that have not been addressed before; or if they have, perhaps you realize it is time to re-evaluate them because you made the decisions when you were a couple.

Just as I have found out "one size does not fit all" so "one answer does not fit all" circumstances. In view of that, I have listed a few.

What about government aid? Is it scriptural to apply for it?

> ...the wealth of the sinner is laid up for the righteous (Proverbs 13:22(b) NKJV).

> For God gives wisdom and knowledge and joy to a man who is good in His sight; but to the sinner He gives the work of gathering and collecting, that he may give to him who is good before God... (Ecclesiastes 2:26 NKJV).

Both of the scriptures above shows us that God gives work and wealth to those who are not believers, and then either directly or indirectly opens the door to provide the shortfall for someone less fortunate. This could be a neutral relationship between the parties, such as through the taxes we all pay. Their taxes might be used to provide a program a single mother can benefit from.

The way I look at this is: "Is it a lifestyle or a stop gap to get you over the hump?" If temporary, then I think it is appropriate scripturally to apply for school meals, food stamps, medical care, and/or monthly assistance, with the idea in mind that it will be short-term and therefore, without guilt.

Should my child go to a secular or Christian school?

I think the less you can upset what their routine was prior to the separation, the better.

Should I make a will or not?

As a single mom, you probably do not have this on your radar, though you should. If something were to happen to you, who do you want raising your children? That is the bottom line. If the other parent is unable or unwilling to, you need to consider who else would. This may not be a comforting thought to contemplate—that you might not be there for them until they are 18; all the same, it is a reasonable consideration.

Should I go to work or not?

Part of this will depend on your financial situation. If possible, especially immediately following the initial upset, I would recommend not going to work, but instead, working part-time or working at home while they are in school. Again, the less you can upset the child's routine, the better. The decision might be to wait before going to work. There is no definite answer for this in the Bible. You need to consider that the time away from them means you will be influencing them less if you go to work, and someone else will be influencing them more. If finances prevent you from staying home, consider carefully who is going to spend all that time with them. You want that person to have the same value system you have, and you want them to love your child, not just take care of them because it is their business. I have seen too many mothers, married or single, "plug the hole" regarding child care with just anyone available, giving their career priority over their children. Of course, if finances dictate differently, you will not have a choice.

What about moving?

Again, for the child's sake, the less you can disturb their previous routine, the better. On the other hand, sometimes it might be better if you were to move closer to family for support.

Should you live with another single mother?

I have seen this work out very well in some instances and not so well in others. In today's economy, it might help financially; however, another factor to be aware of is that you will each discipline your children differently. Just the styles of discipline could cause a lot of conflict. Be sure you know who you are moving in with and have had a discussion first about how you will handle this and other potential issues. Beforehand, you should make sure you both are already handling your finances wisely or one of you may wind up "holding the bag." Another thing to consider is how they keep house. In general, their personal habits and their children's habits will be a model either negatively or positively for your children. Are you on the same page?

What about income changes in general?

Usually a single mother has to tighten her belt. That is just life, but it is not the end of the world. Do not depend on alimony or spousal support. Statistics show it is not always forthcoming.[32] And when these expectations are not met, bitterness can set in. In view of those statistics, become proactive. If possible, set up your finances in such a way that you do not have to depend on the other parent to keep you from being evicted or unable to feed your child.

If you seek Him, God will guide you in all these instances.

NEVER MARRIED?

The single mother who has never been married or lived with a man probably needs basic instruction in budgeting, cleaning, cooking, organization, and schedules. One by-product is that children thrive on schedules and consistency. Another advantage is that God will use all these disciplines to prepare you for marriage. The following proverb gives practical advice for a well-balanced lifestyle whether you ever marry or not. So, if you do desire to marry a Godly man, the best Biblical model for becoming a Godly woman is outlined in Proverbs 31 below.

Who can find a virtuous wife? For her worth is far above rubies. The heart of her husband safely trusts her, so he will have no lack of gain.

She does him good and not evil all the days of her life. She seeks wool and flax, and willingly works with her hands. **[She is a seamstress.]**

She is like the merchant ships; she brings her food from afar. **[She does her own shopping.]**

She also rises while it is yet night, and provides food for her household, and a portion for her maidservants. She considers a field and buys it; from her profits she plants a vineyard. **[She is like a real estate agent and is also a businesswoman, wise in investing.]**

She girds herself with strength, and strengthens her arms. **[She keeps herself healthy.]**

She perceives that her merchandise is good, and her lamp does not go out by night. **[She is diligent because she has confidence in what she is selling.]**

She stretches out her hands to the distaff, and her hand holds the spindle. **[She is one who quilts or does handiwork.]**

She extends her hand to the poor; yes, she reaches out her hands to the needy. **[She considers others less fortunate than herself.]**

She is not afraid of snow for her household, for all her household is clothed with scarlet. [She does not worry about

> *tomorrow because she knows where her children and husband stand spiritually.]*
>
> *She makes tapestry for herself; her clothing is fine linen and purple.* **[She makes her own clothing and dresses to keep up with the times.]**
>
> *Her husband is known in the gates, when he sits among the elders of the land. She makes linen garments and sells them, and supplies sashes for the merchants. Strength and honor are her clothing; she shall rejoice in time to come. She opens her mouth with wisdom, and on her tongue is the law of kindness. She watches over the ways of her household, and does not eat the bread of idleness. Her children rise up and call her blessed; her husband also, and he praises her: Many daughters have done well, but you excel them all. Charm is deceitful and beauty is passing, but a woman who fears the LORD, she shall be praised. Give her of the fruit of her hands, and let her own works praise her in the gates (Proverbs 31:10-31 NKJV).*

None of us are superwomen, and none of us will be able to do all these things, or even most of them all the time. Regardless, this is God's ideal for becoming a virtuous woman and a target for you. These principles serve as a guide for Godly wives and mothers, and are good preparation for marriage too.

In God's foresight, as you are developing into who God wants you to be, your winsomeness will become more obvious to the opposite sex at the same time.

The Book of Ruth is an excellent example of a love story that encompasses Ruth serving her mother-in-law, Naomi. Over a period of several seasons, Boaz notices Ruth's servant attitude and her caring character and is drawn to her. Be a Ruth, going about your daily business faithfully, and God will draw that man He has intended for you, to you. At the risk of sounding old-fashioned, let him find you.

> *He who finds a wife finds a good thing, And obtains favor from the LORD (Proverbs 18:22 NKJV).*

This verse speaks of a *man* finding a wife. That indicates to me that *he* is the one who is looking.

If you are intentionally looking for the man *you* think you want, your priorities may need to be changed. What you think *you need* might not be what you and your child truly need. God is the one who knows what you need. Our hearts deceive us, and if your emphasis is on finding a man, you may not be reflecting Christ. A woman who reflects Jesus is an attraction to a man who is looking for that kind of woman.

> **HANDY HINT for any single woman:** If a man is interested, he'll be drawn to you like bees to honey.

PERSONAL MINISTRY OF SINGLE MOMS

We all want to know what God's will for our lives is. For a single mother, God's will for you is caring for your child, first and foremost. Consider this scripture.

> *Keep watch over yourselves and all the flock of which the Holy Spirit has made you overseers (Acts 20:28(a) NIV).*

You are now the sole overseer in your home. This is probably not what you envisioned for yourself when you became a mother. Nevertheless, you are *it* now. Even though Paul is addressing the church elders, this also applies to you because you are the overseer of your flock (children). You have the main responsibility of your child, and it is an important and unique role ordained by God. Remember, it is not by default because God knew before the foundation of the world that you were going to be a single mother. This is your first ministry. It is your daily destiny, and He wants you to succeed at it. You cannot lose if you consult Him and His Word; He will guide you every step of the way.

As you begin to realize your new role and you adjust to your new set of circumstances, God gives you a period of grace. From my experience and observation, this period of grace comes to you *supernaturally*. This understanding of your new role as a single mom does not necessarily come on the day you go to court or the day the other parent left or died. These feelings cannot be projected onto an expected timeframe, entered on a calendar or put on paper. One day you are suddenly made aware, by the Lord's impression in your heart, that you are the head of your house and accountable to Him alone, and that you are no longer accountable to the other parent. This can present a paradox. You may receive a great release; and yet, a spiritual weight or burden may come in addition to that release when you realize the seriousness of knowing you are solely responsible for your child, never alone, yet responsible in a new way.

As the overseer of your child, it is your first responsibility to feed them spiritually so that no one will be able to deceive your child or ensnare them in any way.

I recall the first time when the Lord ministered to me that I was now accountable to Him and Him alone, that I was no longer answerable to my ex-husband in the same way I was when I was married. There was a freedom that happened supernaturally, but the accountability factor had changed too, and I was now being held responsible by the Lord Himself for my actions. Just like in the world of wholesale, there was no longer a middle man. God had loaned my children to me, and I was responsible to Him for how I raised them.

In I Samuel 1:28, Hannah speaks about her son, Samuel, being lent to her by God.

> *Therefore also I have lent him to the LORD; as long as he lives he shall be lent to the LORD (I Samuel 1:28 NKJV).*

It is the same for us. This is something we need to always keep in the forefront of our minds. They are not ours to keep. Our children are lent to us by the Lord, and they are our number one stewardship and ministry.

> *Lo, children are an heritage of the LORD: and the fruit of the womb is his reward (Psalm 127:3 KJV).*

When I read this, I realized that whatever my ex-husband did to me was one thing, but what he did to the children was another. I had to protect them from broken promises and disappointments as much as possible. These only cause insecurity and apprehension. A good question to ask yourself is, "Would Jesus do this to your child?" If not, then take action to change the circumstances so your child's expectations will not be dashed again and again.

You may need to be proactive to protect your children from broken visitation promises. If the other parent has said they would come at a certain time and did not come, and this is typical of their lifestyle, you can be ready with an alternative of doing something with your child. When it becomes apparent the other parent is extremely late and has not contacted you that they are on the way, be ready with other plans that would be fun for your child, such as going to the park, going to visit friends, going shopping, or something the child would enjoy to take their mind off the fact that the other parent did not show up.

I talked earlier about the "swinging door syndrome." I have seen many women let the partially-absent parent come and go without regard to the detrimental effect it has on the children. He says he is sorry, and as a result she lets him return, only to have him leave again. This becomes a vicious cycle and should be avoided. It is the same mindset as the woman who allows herself to be abused over and over again even though her partner promises never to abuse her again. However, in this case, you must consider the children's needs above your own.

Along about this time a single mom may need to begin making changes in her social circle if she has not already done so since the other parent left. She needs both married couples and responsible singles who will extend themselves towards her and her children in a wholesome way. A single mom especially needs another friend who is a single mom who can relate to her, but not one who will play the "woe is me" game. There are many wise older women who can fill this role in your life.

Paul speaks to Titus about what these older women's responsibilities are and what they are to teach to the younger women. His instructions to the younger women apply to single moms too, and it is good training whether or not she ever marries.

Chapter 6

> ...teach the young women to be sober, to love their husbands, to love their children, to be discreet, chaste, keepers at home, good, obedient to their own husbands, that the word of God be not blasphemed (Titus 2:4-5 KJV).

This was also motivation for me to personally apply these attributes in my life. Because Jesus said He was my husband in Isaiah 54:5, then I could expect He would provide for me like a husband.

> For your Maker is your husband, The Lord of hosts is His name; and your Redeemer is the Holy One of Israel; He is called the God of the whole earth (Isaiah 54:5).

Since I thought about Him in this way, I was motivated to do the things mentioned above, such as fix nutritious meals, keep a clean house, live a Godly life, etc. just as if I were married and wanting to please an earthly husband. Granted, it was my children who benefited immediately and practically, although it was also future preparation for me if I was to remarry. Being single is not a time to kick back. This is a time of preparation for what the Lord has in store for you. You do not know whether you will marry or not. For that reason, in the interim, love your children, live a virtuous, discreet life, and keep your home in order. If you incorporate these things into your life, you will be a good model for your children to follow.

When writing to Timothy, Paul talks about how everyone should treat mothers regardless of age, as well as how the church should view supporting an older widow who does not have a blood family. In addition, He speaks of ways an older widow and a single mother are supposed to conduct themselves. These traits are a good challenge to exhibit for any mother, whether or not her children still live with her. Read his instructions in I Timothy 5.

> Treat the older women as you would your mother, and treat the younger women *[which also includes single mothers]* with all purity as your own sisters. Take care of any widow who has no one else to care for her. But if she has children or grandchildren, their first responsibility is to show godliness at home and repay their parents by taking care of them. This is something that pleases God very much. But a woman who is a

> *true widow, one who is truly alone in this world, has placed her hope in God. Night and day she asks God for help and spends much time in prayer. But the widow who lives only for pleasure is spiritually dead.* **[This includes single mothers.]**
>
> *Give these instructions to the church so that the widows you support will not be criticized. But those who will not care for their own relatives, especially those living in the same household, have denied what we believe. Such people are worse than unbelievers. A widow who is put on the list for support must be a woman who is at least sixty years old and was faithful to her husband. She must be well respected by everyone because of the good she has done. Has she brought up her children well? Has she been kind to strangers? Has she served other Christians humbly? Has she helped those who are in trouble? Has she always been ready to do good?* (I Timothy 5:2-10 NLT).

In verse 10, in the KJV, "being kind to strangers" is called "washing the saints' feet." Paul refers to "washing the saints' feet" as a way to humbly serve others. I like this picture of washing another person's feet. Being humble is an attitude of the heart. True humility is not something you can fake. It is a work of the Holy Spirit. How do you wash the saints' feet?

It also describes a Godly lifestyle which is about your present vision, and it is a significant vision too. Believe me, living this type of lifestyle will bring you more joy than if you live your life for yourself.

Paul continues with instruction to the younger widows which also includes single mothers.

> *The younger widows should not be on the list, because their physical desires will overpower their devotion to Christ and they will want to remarry.* **[The "list" refers to the criteria a local church uses to decide who it should support physically.]**
>
> *Then they would be guilty of breaking their previous pledge* (I Timothy 5:11-12 NLT).

In the KJV, in verse 11, the phrase "their devotion to Christ" is translated "wax wanton," referring to the younger women's desire for Jesus fading. I like that particular wording, "wax wanton" for the reason that it is a stronger description, which in the Greek means "to act voluptuously against." To me, "waxing wanton" is a great picture of a candle that was once hot, burning brightly, and over time starts to flicker and fade; and when the flame went out, the wax dripped down and became cold and hardened. Over and over I have seen young women once on fire for God exchange their desire for Christ into a desire for a man, and I have watched their love for Jesus grow cold. When this happens, it is very sad to me because you can have both, love for Jesus and love for a husband, only in the proper order.

Paul continues:

> *And if they are on the list, they will learn to be lazy and will spend their time gossiping from house to house, meddling in other people's business and talking about things they shouldn't (I Timothy 5:13 NLT).*

This was something I observed when young mothers had too much spare time. How easy it is to slip into too much talking that is unproductive which turns into gossip.

Paul goes on:

> *So I advise these younger widows to marry again, have children, and take care of their own homes. Then the enemy will not be able to say anything against them (I Timothy 5:14 NLT).*

Paul's desire for the younger widows is to remarry and have children. This could include single mothers, too.

Statistics indicate 70%+ of remarriages involving children end in dissolution within 5 1/2 years.[33] In view of these statistics, it seems like a paradox to me, that God, who loves and created families, would like the younger women to remarry and have more children, and yet at the same time, He is fully aware that a step-parenting or blended family situation brings with it new issues. Verse 14 regarding marriage or remarriage is a good desire, yet it is a future vision for you and should not be your first desire.

Paul continues:

> *If a woman who is a believer has relatives who are widows, she must take care of them and not put the responsibility on*

the church. Then the church can care for widows who are truly alone (I Timothy 5:16 NLT).

There are dual instructions here. Did you catch it? Not only is the church commanded to treat widows and single mothers in a certain way (verse 16), but the single mothers are commanded to act in certain ways too (verse 14).

I Kings 17 has a story about a single mother with one son who was almost out of food, to the point of even preparing the final meal so she and her son could die. Have you ever felt that desperate, desperate enough to die and even for your child to die too? God knew this woman's heart and intervened. He spoke to this widow first, to prepare her for an unusual visitor He was going to send to her, named Elijah.

> *Then the word of the LORD came to him, [Elijah] saying, 'Arise, go to Zarephath, which belongs to Sidon, and dwell there. See, I have commanded a widow there to provide for you.'* **[God Himself had already directly told her Elijah would be coming and to get ready.]**
>
> *So he arose and went to Zarephath. And when he came to the gate of the city, indeed a widow was there gathering sticks. And he called to her and said, 'Please bring me a little water in a cup, that I may drink.' And as she was going to get it, he called to her and said, 'Please bring me a morsel of bread in your hand.' So she said, 'As the LORD your God lives,* **[She did not acknowledge Elijah's God as her God yet, because she called him 'your' God."]** *I do not have bread, only a handful of flour in a bin, and a little oil in a jar; and see, I am gathering a couple of sticks that I may go in and prepare it for myself and my son, that we may eat it, and die.'* **[She was desperate, at the end of her rope.]**
>
> *And Elijah said to her, 'Do not fear; go and do as you have said, but make me a small cake from it first, and bring it to me; and afterward make some for yourself and your son.' For thus says the LORD God of Israel: 'The bin of flour shall not be used up, nor shall the jar of oil run dry, until the day the LORD sends rain on the earth.' So she went away and did according to the word of Elijah; and she and he and her household ate for many days.* **[We do not know how long "many days" were except that Elijah was still in the immediate area.]**

Chapter 6

> *The bin of flour was not used up, nor did the jar of oil run dry, according to the word of the LORD which He spoke by Elijah. Now it happened after these things that the son of the woman who owned the house became sick. And his sickness was so serious that there was no breath left in him. So she said to Elijah, 'What have I to do with you, O man of God? Have you come to me to bring my sin to remembrance, and to kill my son?' And he said to her, 'Give me your son.' So he took him out of her arms and carried him to the upper room where he was staying, and laid him on his own bed. Then he cried out to the LORD and said, 'O LORD my God, have You also brought tragedy on the widow with whom I lodge, by killing her son?' And he stretched himself out on the child three times, and cried out to the LORD and said, 'O LORD my God, I pray, let this child's soul come back to him.' Then the LORD heard the voice of Elijah; and the soul of the child came back to him, and he revived. And Elijah took the child and brought him down from the upper room into the house, and gave him to his mother. And Elijah said, 'See, your son lives!' Then the woman said to Elijah, 'Now by this I know that you are a man of God, and that the word of the LORD in your mouth is the truth' (I Kings 17:8-24 NKJV).*

This single mother did not know this visitor was going to solve her problem of no food. She also did not know her son was going to become ill later, and actually die. Yet God was already ahead of her. God is always ahead of us too, no matter what our circumstances are. He knew she would become hopeless when her son got sick and died, but Elijah was already on the scene. As a result of obeying God and Elijah, her food increased, and her son was raised from the dead. Her attitude was changed from hopelessness to hope. God wants to exchange your hopelessness to hope too.

Earlier I mentioned in I Timothy 5:10, about being kind to strangers or "washing the saints' feet." That widow blessed Elijah and "washed a saint's feet" by providing him with water, bread and then a cake.

> *If you try to hang on to your life, you will lose it. But if you give up your life for my sake, you will save it (Luke 9:24 NLT).*

This presents another paradox. As a single mother, the natural tendency is to take care of ourselves and our children first, and hang onto our own time, often to the exclusion of serving others. However, it is in giving that we receive, and that is a lesson all children need to learn.

With our lifestyles being so busy, one way of "losing your life" would be to serve in some way within the church or community. There are a lot of opportunities to volunteer seasonally at a community event during the holidays. Volunteering exposes children to others who are less fortunate than themselves, and they get a more complete world-view than their day-to-day routine. It will help them become more grateful for what you do for them.

For this stage in your life, it would probably be best to serve in a low-key capacity because your emotions will be unstable and the demands on you will be different than they would be in a position requiring a higher commitment. Find something that interests you, and if it is something where both you and your children can volunteer together, it will help you mentally and you will grow spiritually.

YOUR PERSONAL VISION FOR THE FUTURE

Sooner or later, everyone faces this deep-seated question: What is God's will for my life, or what does God want me to do with my life? All single moms need a personal vision from the Lord which will sustain them during this hard time in their life and to encourage them towards their future destiny. You can choose to have future goals such as: when I get married, when the children are out on their own, or when I get enough money, etc. But be careful! You might be so locked into that mindset that you miss out on the unexpected blessings along the way. God's vision for you might be a detour from what you want. God has a way of changing our hearts to fall in line with His desire for you. *IT IS ALL ABOUT YOUR HEART'S ATTITUDE!*

When I was at this stage in my life, looking for what His will was for me, I read the following verse, and then I made a conscious decision to practice James 1:27 by visiting the widows and orphans in *their* troubles.

> *Pure and genuine religion in the sight of God the Father means caring for orphans and widows in their distress and refusing to let the world corrupt you (James 1:27 NLT).*

The KJV version uses the word "afflictions" instead of "troubles," and in the Greek, "afflictions" means "anguish or being burdened." If that was not a picture of how I felt as a single mom, then I do not know what was: troubled, in anguish, burdened. In reality, it is a picture of other single moms, and it took my eyes off of me.

Yes, Biblically speaking I was a widow because I was divorced and abandoned, and my children were fatherless too, ("orphans" as the Bible describes them). However, instead of expecting others to visit *me* in *my* affliction (take care of *me*, give *me* attention), I realized this was a command for me also. I intentionally stepped out of my comfortable circle and reached out to those who were "afflicted" like me.

As a Christian, I am a part of Christ's universal church. Consequently, I am also commanded to visit other single moms. When I began looking at the situations others were in, do you know what I discovered? I usually found them to be more "afflicted" than I was, either materially, spiritually, or both. Not only are others to reach out to you, but you should be reaching out to other single mothers. If you get your eyes off of yourself, you will become a healthier person.

This vision or goal in James 1:27 does not change with time or circumstances because all the individuals in the church are commanded to practice this until they die or Jesus returns. Regardless of what changes in your future circumstances, this is a vision the Lord has for you, to fulfill your destiny. He wants to give you blessings along the way while you are waiting for any other future goals to be attained.

God, in His infinite wisdom, knows that for your own mental and spiritual well-being you not only need a long-term vision (we all do), you need an immediate and constant vision as well. That is why He says:

> *Where there is no vision, the people perish (Proverbs 29:18(a) KJV).*

As you seek Him, He also shows you what that vision can be, and what He has planned for your life. Your personal vision will begin to unfold step-by-step; however, you have to receive it, take it into your heart, and walk in it for it to become your own. It is easier to guide a moving ship than one that is anchored or tied to the dock.

You might consider creating a personal mission statement, just like you would create a list of your goals. If you do not know what your target is, how will you know when you hit it?

CHAPTER 7

Friends

YOUR PHYSICAL (NON-SEXUAL) NEEDS

If you are like I was, you experience few hugs from adults. It is natural to desire physical contact. Touch is so important, but the physical side of a relationship may be woefully lacking in your life.

When you are alone or with children so much of the time, you need to be appreciated by adults, and hugs are one way to bridge that gap. For starters, I intentionally made myself step out of my comfort zone and started hugging other single moms I already knew. An unexpected by-product was that I was freed up more with the touchy-feely side of my relationship with my own children. However, you may have to take the initiative. I have a friend who wears a badge that says "Professional Hugger."

By intentionally being appreciative in a physically demonstrative way toward other women, I discovered others appreciated me more, and I got hugs back. Hugging is actually fun for me now.

I soon discovered that as I relaxed more with my sisters-in-the-Lord, I was able to receive a hug from my brothers-in-the-Lord much more naturally without skepticism or awkwardness.

Of course, there are appropriate and inappropriate types of hugs between a man and woman. The best way to avoid feeling uncomfortable or to not make the man (or his wife) feel uncomfortable, is to hug sideways. A side hug is acceptable in most circles.

Think about your personal comfort zone. Can you start by stretching it out towards another woman friend?

NEW FRIENDS

You have probably already realized that *couples* who were your friends prior to your becoming a single mother have more than likely fallen by the wayside. Usually in a divorce, your friends who were *couples* and knew both of you, feel uncomfortable and usually drop out of the picture. They may feel they will be forced to take sides and as a result, instead, they opt to just fade away. They do not know how to handle the situation because they related to both of you in a certain role, and now that role is changing. For that reason, expect to lose many of your *mutual* friends, maybe dramatically, or maybe they will just quietly slip away. Very few *couples* will remain in your life to support you as a single person. Do not take it personally. This is not necessarily because they do not like you or think what you are doing is wrong. It may affect *them* adversely, especially if their marriage is shaky, causing *them* to re-evaluate their lives, and that may cause them to withdraw from you.

Only a very mature person or mature couple would be able to continue a relationship with both individuals during and after a divorce. But I have seen it happen. When that couple remains in your life, they can often be a catalyst for a quicker healing.

You may have friends who were not couples with both of you; for example, you had girlfriends you did things with, and he had guy friends he did things with (apart from you). They may stick with you through this, although they still need to be objective as to the other partner. They will want to side with you. To the best of your ability, you need to be careful that you present a true, yet balanced view of the separation, divorce, and all the other parts of this process as you perceive it.

> ...there is a friend who sticks closer than a brother (Proverbs 18:24(b) NKJV).

Ideally, you will have previously established several friendships in your life that will fill this role. As you go forward, you will make new friends. During this process and even after all seems settled, you will need people around you who have known you and have seen your track record during the time you were married. These people will have a more complete picture of you and your situation than a new friend. Since you have been influenced negatively by the world and your "ex," you have probably forgotten what you were like *way back when*. They will encourage you and remind you what you were like before becoming a parent and perhaps even before marriage. Their observations of you are more objective than yours alone.

Let me remind you, you cannot do this by yourself. Your best friend is Jesus. He does not want you to walk this path alone. He is on call 24/7. His phone line is never busy or disconnected. He knows all the facts, sees all the different sides, and can guide you in the correct way. Cultivate a friendship with him. Talk to him, and spend time in his presence. He does not want you to carry this burden alone. Jesus said:

> *You are My friends if you do whatever I command you. No longer do I call you servants...but I have called you friends... (John 15:14-15 NKJV).*

Even single friends you had previously are probably not still in your life. In order to remain balanced and heal in a well-rounded way, it is your responsibility to find new friends.

> *A man who has friends must himself be friendly... (Proverbs 18:24(a) NKJV).*

Please notice this verse does not say "Be friendly, and then you will gain friends." It says "has friends." This is in the past tense. In other words, this man has friends already, yet he continues to cultivate them. To have friends, you must be a friend. This is often hard to do when going through the crisis or series of crises like a single mother experiences. Drawing back, rather than investing in friends sometimes seems easier, but it is not wise. Relationships are work, and relationships are a two-way street. You must reach out to others to have friends yourself. This applies to those of the same sex and opposite sex.

If you have tried to fit into the single lifestyle, you probably have found that it does not work too well. Their lifestyle is more spontaneous than yours because you have the needs of your child to attend to.

Be smart! Re-assess your situation. Look around you. Can you find one couple you can incorporate into your lifestyle? What about a support group that has both couples and singles in it? If you are already divorced, a single parents' group is a good place to start.

Chapter 7

Make a list of activities or hobbies you did prior to having a partner or children. Do those things still interest you? Can you incorporate them into your present lifestyle with children? Share that list with a group if you have one. That will encourage you. I did that, and as I have shared my list with others, I have been surprised that some of them wanted to do some of those same things or at least wanted to make their own list.

Now think of things you have always wanted to do, but have not been able to for some reason. I started my list when I was a single mother, and I called my list the "What I want to do when I retire" list. Some people call it their "bucket list," things they want to do before they "kick the bucket." Somehow "kick the bucket" sounded so negative to me, and as I have grown older, I figured out why. I realized I did not want to wait to do those things until I retire or even get close to "kicking the bucket." Why wait until I am retired when I may be too unhealthy to do those things? As a result, I started doing those things and scratching them off my "What I want to do when I retire" list. I found it to be very rewarding. Here are some of them.

I wanted to learn to play the harp. I found out after one semester that this was not for me. It was too expensive, and the harps were too big to haul around easily by myself. But I was able to check it off — √.

I had aspired to play the bagpipes, so I bought a practice chanter. However, when I read the instructions, I learned that bagpipes are moist inside and a great place for mold to grow. Since I was allergic to mold, that stopped me dead in my tracks. But I still checked it off — √.

I also wanted to learn how to yodel. I took an adult education class for a semester and learned how — √.

There are still some things on my list. I desire to go to Israel — still pending. I want to learn to snorkel — still pending. I want to swim with the manatees — still pending.

Now you do not have to be as elaborate as I was, so here are some other ideas:

Cake decorating classes, riding a bike, dancing, swimming, horseback riding, voice lessons, quilting, calligraphy—whatever interests you. Maybe you used to do some things before becoming a parent, and you can pick them up again, or maybe there are new things you want to learn in your life. Lessons do not have to be formal or costly. Perhaps you have a friend that is an expert in something you want to learn, and they would be willing to get you set up and help you get started.

Once your list is made, share it with someone. That will give you courage and accountability. Besides, it is contagious. Others will want to follow your lead.

Can you embark on any one of these things?

OPPOSITE SEX RELATIONSHIPS (OTHER THAN DATING)

Often after a divorce, a single mother will either withdraw from the opposite sex or become promiscuous. If a single mother has swung to the side of having no friends of the opposite sex, this is not good. Often this is because of a fear of pain developing through intimacy again with someone of the opposite sex. To overcome these obstacles, it is wise to develop friends of the opposite sex by being in groups where there are married couples as well as singles.

A good idea is to develop at least one good non-physical, spiritual relationship with a man whose counsel you can trust. A variety of male relationships would be even better for the reason that men and women see things differently, and this is another way the Lord might heal you. This is especially important if the single mother has become bitter towards the opposite sex in general. Establishing a *safe platonic* relationship may be difficult to do. Nevertheless, it is still a healthy goal to strive towards.

As a single person, the best foundation is to be friends first. Then if a romance develops, the foundation will be strong. If not, you may have a lifetime friend and confidante. Ideally, you will share the same faith and do joint ministry together. You may share prayer needs, although here is a word of caution. It is best to share these needs in a group situation because prayer is not only a *spiritual* act, it is an *intimate* act too. When prayer times occur privately between two people of the opposite sex on a regular basis, it gives Satan the opportunity to deceive either one or both into thinking the relationship is developing into something more serious than it really is.

> **PERSONAL EXAMPLE:** During the time I was a single mother, I was involved in groups with both singles and couples that met weekly. Many of the men were my friends, and sometimes, I would ask their advice. I was very careful that whenever I spoke to the married men, at the very least, we had his wife's permission, his wife was in the room, or even better, we included her in our conversations.

If the above is a situation which might occur with you, be sure to always honor the established boundaries of never being alone with a man. That way, you will always fulfill the following scripture:

Abstain from all appearance of evil (I Thessalonians 5:22 KJV).

As friends of the opposite sex, except for sexual desires, we can meet each other's needs, and balance each other out. The best foundation to any friendship should be based on prayer, spiritual discussions, or even reading the Word together.

Single Mom??? What Now???

CHAPTER 8

Children

CHILDREN'S SPECIAL ISSUES

The most precious, priceless relationship you will ever be entrusted with is your child.

Rules without relationships equal rebellion, so you must intentionally develop a relationship with your child that includes rules. This may seem like strange advice, yet I have seen many single mothers so wrapped up in their own lives that they forget the child needs a relationship with them, too. Do not allow yourself to become detached from your children as a result of your own hurts. This is a time when you might tell yourself that you deserve to focus on yourself. This is a snare you must guard against because it is a lie. You will reap long-term consequences if you withdraw into yourself to the exclusion of your children. By the same token, you will reap long-term benefits if you proactively develop a lifestyle that includes your child.

Remember you are preparing your son for a wife or your daughter for a husband. You will do everyone a favor if you teach your children the things you wish your "ex" had learned. Sons need to learn how to respect women and help around the house. Your daughter will probably get married, and there is a man out there somewhere just for her. Teach her to respect herself and how to run a household, including budgeting and finances.

Be aware of praising your children by giving them compliments exclusively for their looks or behavior; a better option is to praise them for their inner characteristics, rather than for a task.

Some good books I would recommend on this topic are:
<u>The Strong Willed Child</u>, by Dr. James Dobson
<u>Bringing Up Boys</u>, by Dr. James Dobson
<u>Bringing Up Girls</u>, by Dr. James Dobson

CHILDREN ASKING WHY

Children need reassurance that the reason their other parent is no longer with them is not their fault. They will feel abandoned and probably rejected no matter what you say or do, even if they do not express it visibly or verbally. Therefore, you cannot stress enough to them that the reason the other parent is not there has nothing to do with them. They do ask the question, "Is it my fault?" even if silently.

No matter what age the child, or circumstances surrounding the situation, any child can understand that the reason the other parent is not living with them any more is because:

(1) He/she chose not to live the way we are living (if that is true and they left); or

(2) He/she did not want to live the way we feel Jesus wants us to (only if it is true that the other parent departed for spiritual reasons).

The hurt will still rise up and expose itself in different degrees at different times; however, this will help reassure them that it is not their fault and hopefully lessen or remove their burden of guilt.

CHILDREN'S CURIOUSITY ABOUT THE OTHER PARENT

Children are naturally curious, but answering their questions about their other parent might be painful for you. Always be open to their questions. Set your issues and feelings aside for a short moment, take a deep breath, and answer any questions they pose. Each question should get an answer which will match their maturity level. The depth to which you answer their questions will have different details at different times depending on their age and experiences. Resist the temptation to over answer or answer in such a way that you are making the other parent out to be the bad guy. If you just answer briefly, yet factually, the child usually will be satisfied. Remember the section about "Stress" and Dr. Yamamoto's advice that a child often misinterprets situations. If you ignore them, or do not give them an answer at all, they will either continue hammering you, or they will make up their own answer, regardless of whether or not their own perspective is true.

In considering your child's feelings, be pro-active in the way you handle their *future* curiosity. A child may be too young or may not be able to verbalize questions about their natural parent. Nevertheless, just like an adopted child, there will come a time in their future when they will want to know more about their other parent. For that reason, it is wiser to put away all home movies, pictures, scrapbooks, videos, etc. of the other parent, rather than destroying them. Simply put them away until the child asks about them. If they are old enough, let them know you have saved those things for them when they grow up, but explain to them that it is too painful for you to have them out as reminders during this time in your life. That way, if they want to look at them in the future, they will know those memoirs are accessible to them. However, if you make the decision unilaterally that you want to get rid of all those memories by destroying them, it may cause a rebound effect between you and your child years later. Your child may want to know what his other parent looked like, or maybe your child will recall a memory and want to see *that picture* again. If you save that part of *their* life, it has the potential for the child to feel, perhaps even unconsciously, that the foundational part of their life is still there as opposed to them feeling as though they were being thrown away, ignored, or not valued.

CHILDREN'S SALVATION

There is a situation that I have seen crop up a lot even among Christians who are married, but it is much more pronounced with Christian single moms. We all have a responsibility to teach our children about salvation. Our children are not automatically saved. There are no grandchildren in God's kingdom. Our children do not have a relationship with the Lord until they personally ask Him to come and live in their hearts by faith. Our children imitate us because they want to please us. If left on their own, their corrupt little hearts would soon draw them away. That is why it is up to us as their parents to teach them the basic doctrines and not forget that they are not saved just because we are. For instance, you may be teaching them songs, scriptures, the Lord's Prayer or the 23rd Psalm. Nevertheless, keep in mind that they are saved the same way we were, by being born again. Until they make their own decision to follow Jesus, they are copying your faith. That is why it is important to walk the walk, and at the same time, keep in mind that they need to accept Jesus for themselves. Ask the Lord for teachable moments.

MUTUAL ROLE MODELS FOR THE SINGLE MOTHER AND CHILD

A wise single mother will develop relationships with others who know you and your child mutually. Choose at least one person you admire who knows your child and who your child knows as well and feels comfortable with. Mutual role models are important for all children as well as for you. They can be a good peer counselor for you as well as for your child at any age. This is a good hedge of protection, especially if you have an older child.

If you have a confrontation with your child that cannot seem to be resolved, or they think is unfair, you can suggest they go to your adult friend for counsel. If this person knows both you and your child well and has the same Christian base, it will help you to rest secure in the knowledge they will give Godly advice, minister appropriately, and not undermine you and your decisions. They may be able to comfort your child and perhaps they can be a real peacemaker at a time when it is really needed. If the child is older, it would be best if you and your child could share those problems with the same person. By them knowing both you and your child intimately, they can more objectively see both sides of a situation. The trick is to have this relationship in place prior to any problems developing. The time to begin developing that type of relationship is now. Ask the Lord who in your immediate circle might be a good candidate for this role.

Parents who do not do this may find that sooner or later the problem(s) may escalate, and they will have to go to professional counseling, which is costly and very time consuming to say the least.

A word to the wise: If the person tells your child the same thing you have been trying to enforce, do not say "I told you so." Just rejoice that God has used someone to get your point across.

Often the problems that arise in family life can be dealt with initially on a peer or layperson level. Many problems are simply communication problems and probably do not require professional counseling. Of course, if it is warranted, then professional counseling is the next step.

ROLE MODELS/BIG BROTHERS/BIG SISTERS FOR THE CHILD

Our children copy us whether we recognize that or not. As they get older, they become more like us, both the good and bad. I wanted mine to reflect my good qualities, and I wanted to be a good model for them.

This was driven home to me one day when I realized my son copied more than just me.

> **PERSONAL EXAMPLE:** As my son grew into his teens, his clothing styles were beginning to change. I knew what he liked, but I had no clue that he was watching the men in the church and how they dressed until one day, when we went shopping, he said he wanted to get some dress pants like our pastor.

One privilege you have as a single mom is to pray for God to send you the perfect adult male or female role model or models for your children. It will not necessarily be only one role model since the needs of your child will change. There might be more than one role model during the same time, or there may be several over a longer period of time to meet the different needs in your child as they grow. Ask the Lord to give you spiritual eyes to recognize this person or persons. It might not necessarily be someone you would seek out because your child's needs are different than yours. That is why you should not limit the Lord in who He might send to you. In fact, you might ask the Lord for spiritual eyes to see how He has already provided for you.

A word to the wise, however, as a Christian, I think you should try to be "equally yoked" in these roles. If possible, I think all role models such as babysitters, volunteers in a "Big Brother/Big Sister Program," and even caregivers should be Christians. They may be spending as much or more accumulative time with your child than you are, especially if you work full-time. Their values will rub off and be communicated and caught by your child whether directly or indirectly. Why spend time explaining and unraveling influences and questions from an "anti" Christian or immoral base if you can avoid it in the first place?

In addition, I think anyone wanting to spend time investing in your child should make a commitment to both of you to avoid your child being let down. For a season, this person is their present security. The commitment could be weekly for two hours, once a month, or whatever you agree upon. That person needs to know your child will depend on them, which is why the time commitment needs to be clear to you and them, as well as your child. They need to understand that your child has been let down and in many ways abandoned or rejected through the separation and divorce process, and your child does not need another adult in their lives who will be unreliable. As a role model, they need to be faithful and responsible to be there when they say they are going to be. Moreover, this teaches responsibility and accountability to the person volunteering their time.

> **PERSONAL EXAMPLE:** I'd been alone about three months, when I realized my son needed a role model. So I began praying. Within the week, as I visited a pharmacy and was waiting for a prescription to be filled, a policeman was sitting there who initiated a conversation with my son. He showed him his night stick, gun and badge. Although it was just a few minutes, this stranger took the time to relate to my son on a "male" level. I know this was the Lord answering my prayer in a small way. Later the Lord provided neighbors and a Big Brother program at our church.

DISCIPLINING CHALLENGES

I have noticed that most single moms are soft touches when it comes to disciplining their children. They carry guilt more than if they were married, especially if they have to work. They usually give in more to the child since a woman's emotions are softer than a man's, and they do not have the emotional backup they need. However, God is your emotional backup.

If you read the following scriptures keeping in mind that "father" is God, then you will understand that God wants all His children (that includes you) to be a blessing and not a grief to Him.

> *A foolish son is the ruin of his father (Proverbs 19:13(a) NKJV).*

> *A foolish son [is] a grief to his father, and bitterness to her who bore him (Proverbs 17:25 NKJV).*

> **PERSONAL EXAMPLE:** When my son was about 4 years old, he was given a pair of cowboy boots that had pointed toes. Foreseeing a possible problem, I told him that if he kicked anyone with them, I'd take them away. Sure enough, within hours, he kicked another child. So I put them up high in his closet where he could "view" them and thereby remember what he did that was wrong and reap the consequences of not being able to wear them.

As a single mom, I did not want my children to be a grief to God, to me or to others. I wanted to be proud of them. Deep down, I think most parents feel that way too.

Children reflect your walk with the Lord. They are your "fruit." When I was out of order with God, such as in a bad mood, or in rebellion, it would filter down to my children. They would be stubborn or rebellious to me and others. Your child's behavior is often a mirror of your life. Be alert as to how they are "acting out." Then watch for how you may be modeling or fueling that action, and take steps to remedy it.

Satan will tell you that any disciplining is fruitless, especially spanking. Or he will try to convince you that spanking is brutal discipline, even calling it child abuse. Therefore, a lot of single moms do not spank, or spank so softly that it does not do any good. Besides, a screaming child will usually cause a single mom to lighten up. This is one way a child manipulates.

It is better to be stricter when they are younger, then as they get older and are showing more responsibility, you can let go little by little. If you let your young child run you ragged and run the household by their demands and actions, when they become teenagers and you try to crack down, they will rebel more than if it is the other way around.

The Word warns against letting a child go undisciplined. A single mother, especially, often fears her child will reject her. This seems to be more of an issue with a single mom than a single dad. Parenting is not a popularity contest. If a single mother is secure in the Lord and has a good self-image based on God's Word, she will be more effective in disciplining correctly. God's discipline, done correctly, is not child abuse. However, love must be the motive—God's love.

Disciplinary action is done for the *child's* own good, to correct the behavior, not to release your feelings. When you are out of control verbally and/or physically, you should wait until your emotions are under control. You should not discipline your child out of *your* anger. Admittedly, this is harder for some of us than others. An angry parent has already lost the battle before they even start because they have lost control of themselves and the situation. If you are yelling, you have lost control. You can be upset at the act the child has done, but never lose sight of the fact that you are not upset at *who* the child is as a person. It is the behavior that needs to be corrected. This is the principle of hating the sin, but not hating the sinner.

You have a responsibility to teach your child, and one area that needs to be taught is discipline. Your child is going to be disciplined by other authorities in the world, such as a teacher, a store owner, or a policeman, which is why they need to learn responsibility initially at home.

You are given authority by God to spank your child. To ignore them or their actions is a form of neglect. You can be sure your child will test you as soon as someone comes in the house, you get on the phone, or when you are out in public. If you do not let them get away with a certain action at home, do not allow them to act that way when you are out in public. That does not necessarily mean spanking them in public. If you have been consistent in times past, often, just speaking a word of reproof to them, in love, and letting them know that consequences will follow once you are home, should be enough to change their current behavior. The trick for success is that consequences *will* follow. If you let consequences for their inappropriate action slide once you get home, the child will figure out very quickly that you do not mean what you say and will continue to act poorly in public.

A frequent question is: What justifies spanking? Years ago on the radio program "Focus on the Family," I heard Dr. James Dobson say willful defiance is one action that needs to be nipped in the bud. Spanking (not beating) is the most effective way to get the child's attention when they have willfully disobeyed you. Just be sure you go to them afterwards and explain you love *them*, but that you do not like the way they are *acting*. Then give them a hug.

Psychologists say if you are angry when you administer discipline, (whether you discipline them corporally or with a time out, restriction, etc.) usually a child under age of ten or so does not make the logical connection that he is being disciplined because of his act. Instead they think they are being disciplined because you are angry. You must verbally make the logical sequential connection for him by saying something like: "You are going to get a spanking because you (a) hit your sister, (b) lied about ..., or (c) defied me." Or you might say: "You are going to have a time out because you are not sharing your toys."

In the Hebrew language, the word "rod" means a stick used for chastening. This could take the form of either a verbal or physical altercation. A rebuke refers to disciplining by correcting with words. The child may need one or the other or both.

> *The rod and rebuke give wisdom, but a child left to himself brings shame to his mother (Proverbs 29:15 NKJV).*

If you take the time to explain to your child *why* they are being disciplined or spanked, the discipline you administer will become an intentional act done more deliberately out of love, instead of a quick reaction done out of anger. The "why" should never be omitted.

The staff was different. It was used for protection and comfort.

> *Your rod and your staff protect and comfort me (Psalm 23:4(b) NLT).*

If you discipline your child God's way, they will feel protected and comforted because children feel safe when boundaries are established and enforced. For the reason that you are accountable to God for the child He has lent you, God wants to slow you down so you do not abuse them or discipline unfairly.

Although you need to explain why to the child, sometimes an explanation from the child will give you the bigger picture of what happened or how they feel. That explanation may change the type of discipline required.

Not all discipline is spanking. "Time out" works for some children almost all of the time. Nevertheless, some children need stricter or different discipline. You have to figure out what will get their attention enough for them to change their behavior. It may be by trial and error that you discover what kind of consequence will affect them enough so they do not repeat their inappropriate actions. Be alert to the fact that the consequences will change as they get older.

The worst thing I could do to my son (in his eyes), was to make him go to his room and wait for me to come punish him. The wait made him reflect on his actions, and it was the best thing for me as it would calm me down enough to discipline him properly.

As the saying goes, "Let the punishment fit the crime." One common example might be if the child refuses to eat what is on his plate, you remove his plate, do not allow snacking, and make him wait until the next meal. He will probably be hungry enough to eat when the next meal comes around without balking. No spanking needed. The consequences will fit the behavior.

I highly recommend <u>Have a New Kid by Friday</u>, by Dr. Kevin Leman. This book is humorous, and talks about natural consequences for inappropriate behavior, yet it is filled with wisdom, and if consistently applied, really works.

Most parents want their children to have a better life than they had growing up and to become better people than they are. Another reason to correctly discipline your child is because everyone has some kind of reputation among their friends and family, including your child.

> *Even a child is known by his doings, whether his work be pure, and whether it be right (Proverbs 20:11 KJV).*

I personally wanted to have a good reputation among the people I was around, and I wanted my children to have a good reputation too. I did not want my friends and family to dread us visiting as a result of the actions of my children, so this became one of my most frequent prayers as a single mother—that my children would be a delight to be around.

> *Correct your son, and he will give you rest; Yes, he will give delight to your soul (Proverbs 29:17 NKJV).*

Chapter 8

"Delight to your soul" is another way of saying that you can be proud (in a good way) of your child, whether you are in a public setting or privately at home. Correction and consistent discipline done in a loving manner will result in you resting in the fact that your child is behaving the way you want him to, whether or not you are present.

Remember, until a child is born again, they are sinners by nature. You cannot always reason with a young child. You may need to get their attention by spanking. As a child gets older, restricting where it hurts them, not you, is the key. If you restrict a child and it is really *you* on restriction as well, that does not help the situation since you will feel limited too. A restriction should only affect the child. If you are also feeling constrained personally by the restriction you have laid down, and you lessen the restriction, making it easier on the child and yourself, then the next time you try to impose a restriction or time limit of some kind, the child will know he can wear you down and get out of being punished.

You may need to be creative in what the consequences are, and it may be trial and error for awhile.

I have noticed that single mothers fall prey to nagging more than a single dad does. When a single mom has the habit of nagging, they have taught their child to ignore the request the 1st, 2nd or 3rd time, etc. The child knows he will not be disciplined right away, if at all. This is laziness on the part of the parent. It takes time and effort to discipline. Tell the child once what you expect, and explain what the consequences will be. If you do need to tell the child *again* about correcting a certain behavior, that is the time to *consistently* follow through with those pre-determined consequences.

If you ignore your child, you are being selfish and more devoted to yourself and your activities than doing what God expects, and you will reap what you sow.

Over and over I have observed a child taking advantage of a situation when a mother has telephonitis. If she is giving her attention to someone else and ignoring the child, she is setting up a scenario for bad behavior. Even "in-person" conversations with others can be selfish if your child is demanding attention in negative actions.

When you do not pay the proper attention to your child, he may become a whiner. A whining child is trying to get your attention. If he does not get it, he will increase his whining either in volume or in quantity. Teach them to say "excuse me," and then be sure to respond either with words or a motion to wait. Just be sure you do not let them wait so long that they start interrupting again. If you do, you are reinforcing disrespect to your child, indicating to them that they are not important. When you are involved with another person, especially an adult, they need to learn patience and respect for others. This also teaches them that you are not always available to respond to their every whim immediately.

> *Discipline your children while there is hope. Otherwise, you will ruin their lives (Proverbs 19:18 NLT).*

Another thing to remember is that punishment is for the deed. Correction is to prevent future repetition of the deed. This is how God corrects us. Sometimes He smacks our hands (spiritually speaking) for the deed. At other times He corrects us by letting us reap the natural consequences of our actions to teach us not to repeat that action again.

> **PERSONAL EXAMPLE:** When my daughter was about eight, she began lollygagging in the morning, and I was concerned she would be late for school. I tried nagging, and obviously that was fruitless. So I bought her an alarm clock. First I would set it for her, and if she did not get up out of bed when it went off, I reset it. But this did not work either, as she soon realized that I still was more interested in her getting to school on time than she was. Instead, I delegated the setting of her own alarm the night before to her. Then I let her turn it off and get up in the morning without any follow-up from me. This taught her responsibility in stages.

In the example above, my daughter became responsible to get up if she knew she had to walk to school after oversleeping. If you bail your child out, they will not learn the "natural consequences" of their actions. Years ago, I can remember hearing Dr. Dobson on his radio show "Focus on the Family" say that you have to make it their problem. If you are able to transfer what was previously your responsibility to the child's responsibility, you are not "the meanie." They learn personal responsibility instead of reacting to what was previously your action. This is exactly what I did by substituting my constant reminders to hurry and get up, to an alarm clock instead.

No section on discipline would be complete without mentioning the strong-willed child. God knew some of us would have strong-willed children, and I believe He gave us instructions for them specifically in the following verses.

The single mom with the strong-willed child is the target of more "well-wishing advisors" than if she were married with a strong-willed child; and I have noticed it usually comes from people who have no children or who have children with milder temperaments.

The following verse in Ecclesiastics explains why the strong-willed child is the way he is and how to deal most effectively with him.

> *Because the sentence against an evil work is not executed speedily, therefore the heart of the sons of men is fully set in them to do evil (Ecclesiastes 8:11 NKJV).*

It is in his heart's nature to do evil. In view of that, the emphasis is on a quick punishment, rather than a long, drawn-out type of discipline. The more quickly you respond in love, not anger, to bad behavior, the sooner a strong-willed child will realize you are serious and mean business when you say something.

> **PERSONAL EXAMPLE:** At one stage in his life, prior to a spanking, my strong-willed son would try to dissuade me with his screaming and carrying on so I would not spank him. But I knew he was trying to manipulate me. So I decorated a baseboard and painted the following scripture on it.
>
> > *No discipline is enjoyable while it is happening—it's painful! But afterward there will be a quiet harvest of right living for those who are trained in this way (Hebrews 12:11 NLT).*
>
> I would read it to him first, making sure he knew why he was being spanked. Then I would spank him and give him a hug and repeat the explanation of why he was being spanked.

I believe the main reason I see the fruit of righteousness in him now that he is an adult is because I consistently persevered in meting out punishment as it was warranted. It is so easy to give up when you are tired or too busy. Especially with a strong-willed child, you have to be sure to pick your battles.

Some bad behavior is more serious than others. Here is an example of a behavior that started out innocently enough, but grew into something more harmful very quickly.

> **PERSONAL EXAMPLE:** My son used to play "shoot 'em up" cowboys, which to my way of thinking was harmless. But the more he played, the more he got into the character, and I started seeing a mean streak coming out in him. Then a wise woman shared this scripture with me.
>
> > *The LORD examines both the righteous and the wicked. He hates those who love violence (Psalm 11:5 NLT).*
>
> However, I continued to think it was no big deal, he was "just a boy." Then one day he took his play gun, pointed it in my face and said "Bang, you are dead." I immediately realized his imagination had reached a new level of acting out and recognized I needed to take action. Shooting in the air was fine, but selecting a person as a target and verbalizing death was another step in the wrong direction. So I took his gun away from him. Today, one equivalent would be video games that encourage violence and death. If your child watches shows or any other media that encourages violence, you need to recognize how serious it is. Do not be deceived, it will only escalate.

CHAPTER 9

Reflection

A FINAL REFLECTION

Do not sell yourself short; God certainly does not. His promises are timeless. Being a single mother is only *part* of your personal journey; it is not your *entire* journey, and it certainly is not your *final* destiny. By keeping that perspective, this season can be a time of learning so you can pass on the lessons you experience to those who follow behind you, especially your children and other single mothers. If you lean on Him, nothing will be wasted. Even now, if you let Him, He will turn your mourning into dancing and exchange your ashes and sackcloth for true joy in the Kingdom.

> *You have turned for me my mourning into dancing; You have put off my sackcloth and clothed me with gladness, To the end that my glory may sing praise to You and not be silent. O LORD my God, I will give thanks to You forever (Psalm 30:11–12 NKJV).*

Look up! God is not finished with you yet. In place of moaning and mourning your situation, you can receive dancing shoes and become a ballerina in His Kingdom. IT IS YOUR CHOICE!

ENDNOTES

1. http://en.wikipedia.org/wiki/Single-parent_families; http://www.census.gov/apsd/techdoc/cps/cpsmar06.pdf, posting 3/2/10
2. "Focus on the Family," Carrie Tinsley, email dated 3/5/2010
3. http://www.thebondedfamily.com/blendedfamilystatistics, posting 7/2010
4. *TIME Magazine*, "The New American Pocketbook," March 26, 2012, page 33
5. "Focus on the Family," Jim Daly, letter dated June 2012.
6. The Heritage Foundation, Seek Social Justice, page 5, http://www.seeksocialjustice.com/index.php/rethinking-social-justice, posting as of 2009.
7. A nuclear family is a family group consisting of only a father and mother and their children, who share living quarters. http://en.wikipedia.org/wiki/Nuclear_family, posting 3/2/10
8. http://www.blueletterbible.org/lang/lexicon/lexicon.cfm?Strongs=G5503&t-KJV
9. http://www.blueletterbible.org/lang/lexicon/lexicon.cfm?Strongs=H3490&t=KJV and http://www.blueletterbible.org/search/translationResults.cfm?page=2&criteria=fatherless&sf=5&sstr=1&t=KJV
10. Smith, Chuck. "Genesis 37-38." The Word for Today. Blue Letter Bible. 1 Jun 2005. 2012. 6 Aug 2012. <http:// www.blueletterbible.org/commentaries/comm_view.cfm?AuthorID=1&contentID=4735&commInfo=25&topic=Genesis&ar=Gen_38_6 >, posting 8/6/12
11. *Ishmael* means *God hears.*
12. Or *live to the east / of*
13. Or *seen the back of*
14. *Beer Lahai Roi* means *well of the Living One who sees me.*
15. Kaoru Yamamoto is Professor of Educational Psychology at the Graduate School of Education, University of Colorado at Denver, http://www.alibris.com/search/books/author/Yamamoto,%20Kaoru/aid/5531743, posting 8/3/2012

16. http://en.wikipedia.org/wiki/Holmes_and_Rahe_stress_scale, posting 8/10/2010

17. http://en.wikipedia.org/wiki/Holmes_and_Rahe_stress_scale, posting 8/10/2010

18. www.blueletterbible.org/lang/lexicon/lexicon.cfm?Strongs=G2644&t=KJV, posting 1/17/2012

19. http://www.hymnsite.com/lyrics/umh377.sht, posting 7/2/2012

20. http://www.uscj.org/soeast/columbus/mourning_custom.htm, posting 1/30/2012

21. Judith Wallerstein, *The Unexpected Legacy of Divorce Hyperion, 2000*, http://www.acodp.com/char.htm, posting 8/10/2010

22. Smith, Chuck. "Ruth 1-4." The Word for Today. Blue Letter Bible. 1 Jun 2005. 2012. 13 Aug 2012. <http://www.blueletterbible.org/commentaries/comm_view.cfm?AuthorID=1&contentID=6773&commInfo=25&topic=Ruth&ar=Rth_1_1>

23. *The Sunday Peninsula Herald, Peninsula Life,* "'Alone Together' Supports Divorce Recovery," Monterey, CA, Sunday March 3/1/81, Section B

24. Author unknown, *Crisis Counseling*, "The Never-Ending Crisis-Divorce," page 149

25. Author unknown, *Crisis Counseling*, "The Never-Ending Crisis-Divorce," page 143

26. A eunuch is one who is naturally incapacitated either for marriage or begetting children. *Thayer's Lexicon,* http://www.blueletterbible.org/lang/lexicon/lexicon.cfm?Strongs=G2135&t=KJV, posting 8/2/12

27. http://www.thebondedfamily.com/blendedfamilystatistics, posting 8/13/2011

28. http://www.thebondedfamily.com/blendedfamilystatistics, posting 8/13/2011

29. *Beautiful Christian Sister,* Maya Angelou, http://www.gather.com/viewArticle.action?articleId=281474977776516, posting 8/2/12

30. http://www.jewfaq.org/divorce.htm, posting 8/5/12

31 The Art of Thinking Brilliantly, Graham Cooke, http://www.brilliantbookhouse.com, posting 3/2/2012

32 The 2001 proportion of custodial parents receiving every child support payment they were due was 44.8 percent. http://family.findlaw.com/child-support/support-basics/support-stats.html, posting 8/10/10

33 http://www.thebondedfamily.com/blendedfamilystatistics, posting 3/4/2012

www.ingramcontent.com/pod-product-compliance
Lightning Source LLC
Chambersburg PA
CBHW051835090426
42736CB00011B/1815